Egerton Ryerson Young

Oowikapun

How the Gospel reached the Nelson River Indians

Egerton Ryerson Young

Oowikapun
How the Gospel reached the Nelson River Indians

ISBN/EAN: 9783337233303

Printed in Europe, USA, Canada, Australia, Japan

Cover: Foto ©Lupo / pixelio.de

More available books at **www.hansebooks.com**

OR,

𝕳ow the 𝕲ospel reached the ... s.

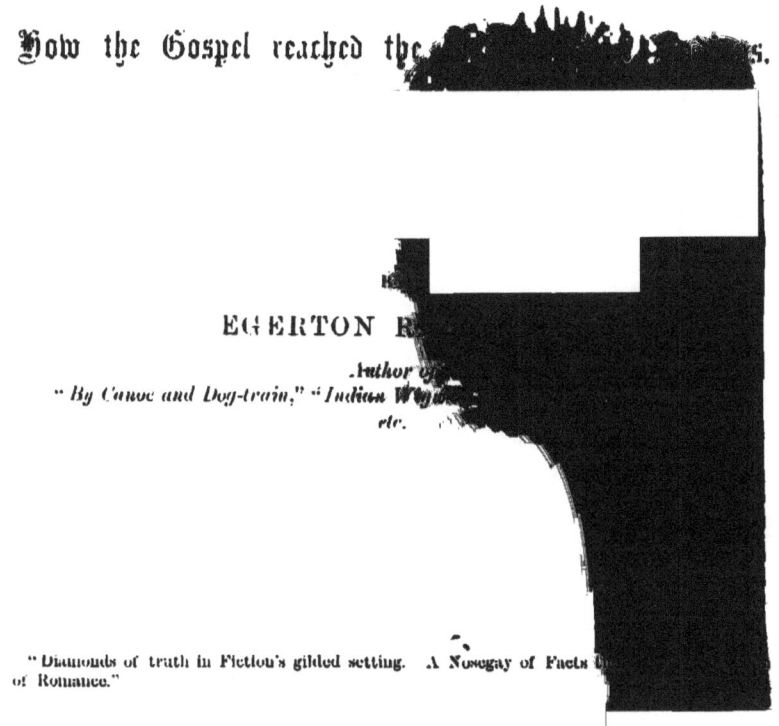

EGERTON R.

Author of
" By Canoe and Dog-train," " Indian Wigwam," *etc.*

" Diamonds of truth in Fiction's gilded setting. A Nosegay of Facts ...
of Romance."

LONDON :
CHARLES H. KELLY, 2, Castle Street, City Road, E.C.,
AND 66, Paternoster Row, E.C.

1895.

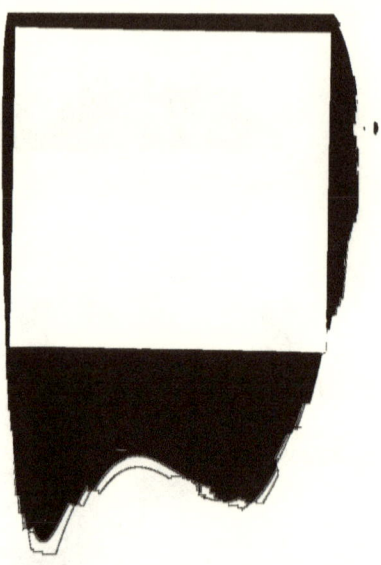

Printed by Hazell, Watson, & Viney, Ld., London and Aylesbury.

CONTENTS.

GLOSSARY OF NAMES.

VARIOUS DIALECTS.

INDIAN.	FREE TRANSLATION.
Oo-wik-a-pun	*One who is longing for light.*
Astumastao	*One who dwells in the sunshine.*
Me-yoo-te-sik	*Bright eyes.*
Sa-gas-ta-o	*Sunrise.*
Me-yoo-achimo-win	*Good news.*
Koo-saf-a-tum	*The conjurer.*
Kis-ta-yim-oo-win	*The man of pride.*
Moo-koo-mis	*The old sage.*

LIST OF ILLUSTRATIONS.

CHAPTER I.

"THE WOLF HAD SEIZED HIS LEFT ARM."

CHAPTER I.

THAT Oowikapun was unhappy, strangely so, was evident to every one in the Indian village. New thoughts deeply affecting him had in some way entered into his mind, and he could not but show that they were producing a great change in him.

The simple, quiet, monotonous life of the young Indian hunter was strangely broken in upon, and he could never be the same again. There had come a decided awakening—the circle of his vision had suddenly enlarged, and he had become aware of the fact that he was something more than he imagined. In his simple faith he had paddled along the beautiful rivers, or wandered through the wild forests of his country, catching the fish or hunting the game, where at times he had heard the thunders crash, had seen the majestic tree riven by the lightning's power, and perhaps in these seasons of nature's wild commotion, had " seen God in the cloud and heard Him in the wind." Yet, until lately, he had never heard of anything which had caused him to imagine that he was in any way allied to that Great Spirit, or was in any way responsible to Him.

What was the cause of this mental disquietude ; of these long hours of absorbing thought ; why did Oowikapun thus act ? To answer these enquiries we must go back a little and accompany him on a hunting trip which he made in the forest months ago.

Hearing from some other hunters of a place where grey wolves were numerous, and being ambitious to kill some of these fierce brutes, that he might adorn his wigwam with their warm skins, he took his traps and camping outfit and set out for that region of country. It was more than two hundred miles away. He soon found tracks in abundance, and ere he made his little hunting lodge in the midst of a spruce grove, he set his traps for the fierce wolves in a spot which seemed to be their rallying place. As they are very suspicious and clever, he carefully placed two traps close together and sprinkled them over with snow, leaving visible only the dead rabbits which served as bait. Then scattering more snow over his own tracks as he moved away, in order to leave as little evidence of having been there as possible, he returned to his tent-like lodge, prepared and ate his supper, smoked his pipe, and then, wrapping himself up in his blanket, was soon fast asleep.

Very early next morning he was up and off to visit his traps. His axe was slipped in his belt, and his gun, well loaded, was carried ready for use if necessary. When he had gotten within a few hundred yards of the place where he had set his heavy traps, he heard the rattling of the chains which were attached to them. This sound, while it made his heart jump, was very welcome, for it meant that he had been successful. When he drew near the traps he found that a fierce old wolf, in trying to get the rabbit from one of them without springing it, had been caught in the other, and although both of his hind legs were held by the sharp teeth of the trap, he had managed to drag it and the heavy log fastened to it quite a distance.

When Oowikapun drew near the wolf made the most desperate efforts to escape; but the strong trap held him securely, and the heavy log on the chain made it impossible for him to get far away.

Oowikapun could easily have shot him, but ammunition was dear, and the bullet-hole in the skin would be a blemish. Then the sound of the gun might scare away the game that might be near, so he resolved to kill the wolf with the back of his axe. Better would it have been for him if he had shot him at once. So putting down his gun, he took his axe out of his belt and cautiously approached the treacherous brute. The sight

of the man so near seemed to fill him with fury, and, unable
to escape, he made the most desperate efforts to reach him.
His appearance was demoniacal, and his howls and snarls would
have terrified any one except an experienced, cool-headed hunter.

Oowikapun, seeing what an ugly customer he had to deal
with, very cautiously kept just beyond the limits of the fearful
plunges which the chain would allow the wolf to make, and
keenly watched for an opportunity to strike him on the head.
So wary and quick was the wolf that some blows received only
more maddened without disabling him.

Oowikapun at length becoming annoyed that he should have
any difficulty in killing an entrapped wolf, resolved to end the
conflict at once with a decisive blow. So with upraised axe he
placed himself as near as he thought safe, and waited for the
infuriated brute to spring at him. But so much force did the
entrapped animal put into that spring that it carried the log
attached to the chain along with him. His sharp, glittering,
fang-like teeth snapped together within a few inches of
Oowikapun's throat; and such was the force of the collision
that the Indian was hurled backwards, and ere he could assume
the aggressive, the sharp teeth of the wolf had seized his left
arm, which he threw up for defence. They seemed to cut down
to the very bone, causing intense pain. But Oowikapun was
a brave and cool-headed man, and a few blows from the keen
edge of the axe in his right hand soon finished a foe whose only
weapons were his sharp teeth. He was soon lying dead in the
snow; but his beautiful skin was almost worthless as a robe
on account of the many gashes it had received, much to the
annoyance of Oowikapun, who had not dreamed of having a
battle so severe.

The traps were soon reset, and Oowikapun, with the heavy
wolf on his back, set out for his camp. As he had set some
smaller traps for minks and martens in a different direction,
he turned aside to visit them. This would cause him to return
to his camp by another trail. While moving along under his
heavy load, he was surprised to come across the snowshoe tracks
of another hunter. He examined them carefully, and decided

that they were made by some person who must have passed along
there that very morning, early as it was.

As the trail of this stranger, whoever he could be, was in the
direction of the traps which Oowikapun wished to visit, he
followed them up, and when he reached his traps found a mink
had been caught in one of them. But the stranger had taken
it out and hung it up in plain sight above the trap on the
branch of a tree. Then the stranger, putting on fresh bait,
had reset the trap.

Of course, Oowikapun was pleased with this, and delighted
that the stranger had acted so honestly and kindly toward him.

Fastening the mink in his belt, he hurried on to his camp as
fast as he could under his heavy load; for his wounded arm had
begun to swell, and was causing him intense pain. His stoical
Indian nature would have caused him to bear the pain with
indifference; but when he remembered how the wolf, maddened
by his capture, had wrought himself up into such a frenzy, and
that his mouth was foaming with madness when he made that
last desperate spring and succeeded in fastening his fangs in his
arm, he feared that perhaps some of that froth might have
gotten into his blood. He understood that unless some remedies
were quickly obtained, madness might come to him, to be followed
by a death most dreadful.

But what could he do? He was several days' journey from
his own village, and many miles from any hunter of his acquaint-
ance. He had, in his vanity, come alone on this hunting
expedition, and now, alone in the woods, far away from his
friends, here he is in his hunting lodge, a dangerously wounded
man.

Fortunately, he had taken the precaution of sucking as many
of the wounds as he could reach with his mouth, and then had
bound a deer-skin thong on his arm above the wounds as tightly
as he could draw it. While brooding over his misfortune, he
suddenly remembered about the snowshoe tracks of the stranger.
He resolved to try and find his lodge and secure help. To decide
was to immediately act. The few preparations necessary were
soon made, and so taking the most direct route to the spot where

he had last seen the trail of the stranger he was soon in it. He
was uncertain at first whether to go backwards or forwards on it
in order to reach the wigwam, for he had not the remotest idea
whether these tracks led to or from it. So his native shrewdness
had to come in play to solve the question. First, he noticed
from the way the snowshoes sank in the snow that the man was
carrying a heavy load. Next, he observed that the tracks were
not like those of a hunter going out from his home, moving about
cautiously looking for game, but were rather those of a man well
loaded down from a successful hunt and pushing on straight for
home with his burden. Quickly had he read these things and
arrived at his conclusions; so he resolved to go on with the trail.
He was not disappointed. He travelled only a few miles ere, in
a pleasant grove of balsam trees, on the borders of a little ice-
covered lake, he discovered, by the ascending smoke from the
top, the wigwam of his unknown friend. Without hesitancy he
marched up to it, and, lifting the large moose skin, which served
as its only door, he stooped down and entered. A pleasant fire
was burning on the ground in the centre, and partly circled
around it was the Indian family. As though Oowikapun had
been long looked for as an expected, honoured guest, he was
cordially welcomed in quiet Indian style and directed to a comfortable place in the circle, the seat of the stranger. The pipe
of peace was handed to him, and but few words were spoken until
he had finished it.

Indian eyes are sharp, even if at times their words are few;
and it was not many minutes before the owner of the wigwam
saw that something was wrong. He drew from him the story of
the killing of the wolf and his fears that perhaps all the froth
from the animal's teeth had not been rubbed off by the leather
shirt and other covering through which they had passed as they
pierced into his arm.

If Oowikapun had travelled a thousand miles he could not
have been more fortunate in the man to whom he had gone.
This man was Memotas, the best Indian doctor in all that vast
country. When his hunting seasons were over he always spent
his time in studying the medicinal qualities of the roots and

herbs of the country which the Great Spirit had created for some good purpose. He then became a benediction to the afflicted ones, receiving but very little fee or reward, as a general thing.

Quickly did Memotas apply his remedies both external and internal, for he knew the risks the man was running; and he gently insisted on the man remaining in his wigwam as his guest for several days, until he was about recovered from his wounds. He would not even hear of his going to visit his traps for fear his blood might become heated by the vigorous exercise, and thus aggravate his wounds. So Memotas himself looked after them, and several times returned with rich spoils of fur-bearing animals, which he gladly handed over to the grateful man.

These great kindnesses completely won the heart of the wounded man, who considered himself most fortunate in finding so kind a friend in his hour of need. The kind-hearted wife of Memotas was also interested in Oowikapun, and did all she could to add to his comfort and hasten his recovery. The injured man had been surprised at the kindness and respect which Memotas constantly manifested toward her, and was amazed that he often asked her advice. He did not as the married men with whom Oowikapun was acquainted treat her unkindly and even consider her inferior to himself, as they treated their wives. While Memotas' wife, whose Indian name was Meyooachimoowin, was very industrious and kept her wigwam and her children tidy and clean, she was never considered merely a drudge and a slave, and left to do all the heavy work. Strange to say, she was not allowed to cut the wood in the forest and then drag it home. Neither did she have to carry the heavy buckets of water up from the lake, as other Indian women were accustomed to do. Nor did she have to go out into the woods, perhaps miles away, and carry home on her back the deer which her husband had shot. Memotas never would allow her to do anything of the kind. He did all this himself, and seemed even anxious to save her from fatigue and toil. Then when the meals were prepared she was not gruffly sent away to wait until the men had eaten, but with them and the children she sat down on terms of perfect equality.

They had two children, a boy and a girl, whom they called

Meyookesik and Sagastao. He noticed that the girl was just as much loved and petted as the boy, and even as kindly treated. This was a state of affairs entirely unknown in the wigwams of the pagan Indians. There the boys are petted and spoiled and early taught to be proud and haughty, and to consider that all girls and women, even their own sisters and mothers, are much inferior to them and only worthy of their kicks and contempt. The boys get the best of everything going and are allowed to eat with the men first, while the poor women and girls have to wait until they have finished and then be content with what is left, which is often not much. Even then they have to struggle with the dogs for these fragments. The result is they are often half starved.

Very few comparatively were the diseases known among the aboriginal tribes of America before the advent of the white man. Their vocation as hunters, however, rendered them liable to many accidents. Possessing no firearms, and thus necessarily obliged to come in close contact with the savage beasts in their conflicts with them, they were often severely wounded. Fortunate is it for the injured one if he has companions near, when the bone is fractured, or the flesh torn.

If the injuries are not considered very desperate, a little camp is improvised, and with a day or two of rest, with some simple remedies from nature's great storehouse, the forest, a cure is quickly effected. If a leg or arm is broken, a stretcher of young saplings is skilfully prepared, interwoven with broad bands of soft bark, and on this elastic easy couch the wounded man is rapidly carried to his distant wigwam by his companions.

When there are but two persons, and an accident happens to one of them, two young trees that are tough and elastic are used. Their tops of small branches are allowed to remain, and very much aid in diminishing the jolting caused by the irregularities of the ground. No carriage spring ever more successfully accomplished its purpose. A couple of crossbars preserve the saplings in position, and the bark of some varieties of shrubs or trees cut into bands and joined to either side forms an even couch. In this way an injured man has often been dragged by his companion for many miles, and in several instances it has been found on his arrival that the fractured bones were uniting, and soon the limb was whole again.

With these simple children of the forest wounds heal with great rapidity, and fractured bones soon unite. This reparative power of the aborigines when injured is only paralleled by the wonderful stoicism with which they bear injuries and inflict upon themselves the severest torture. With flints as substitutes for lances they will cut open the largest abscesses to the very bone. They will amputate limbs with their hunting knives, checking the haemorrhage with red-hot stones—as was done long ago by the surgeons of Europe. With marvellous nerve many a wounded hunter or warrior has been known to amputate his own limb. They were familiar with and extensively used warm fomentations. If rheumatism or other kindred diseases assailed them. the Turkish bath in a very simple form was often used. Sometimes a close tent of deer skins served the purpose. The patient was put in the little tent, while near him heated stones were placed, over which water was thrown until the confined air was heated to the required temperature and saturated with the steam. Sometimes a hole was dug in the ground about eight feet deep. In this the patient was placed, and the same plan adopted as in the wigwam.

Oowikapun had fortunately broken no bones in his battle with the savage wolf, but he knew that his wounds were dangerous. Some of them were so situated in his arm that he could not reach them with his mouth, in order that he might suck out the poisonous saliva of the wolf that he feared might be in them ; and, it now being in the depth of winter, he could not obtain the medicinal herbs which the Indians use as poultices for dangerous wounds of this description.

The following incident also shows the tact and shrewdness with which an Indian can act in an emergency of great difficulty.

On one occasion Judge Upham, of New Brunswick, was travelling in the woods in winter, with an Indian for guide. The snow was so deep and the difficulty of moving so great that the judge became exhausted, and sitting down, he directed the Indian to go and get help, while he remained where he was. The Indian positively refused, but after much persuasion he consented. on condition that the judge should continue to sit on a stump which he pointed out, and if he fell off, should immediately get on again. After some remonstrance the judge was forced to agree to the strange proposition, and make the required promise. He mounted the stump and the Indian disappeared. By-and-by the judge fell asleep, and, as the natural result, tumbled off the stump. Then he understood why the Indian had made him promise to sit on the stump— to prevent him from going to sleep and being frozen to death. When the Indian finally arrived with help, he found the judge sitting on the stump, but with great difficulty keeping awake. He owed the preservation of his life to this simple ruse of the red man.

CHAPTER II.

"OOWIKAPUN SPRANG BACK TO THE NEAREST TREE."

CHAPTER II.

OOWIKAPUN was bewildered at the marvellous contrast between what he had been accustomed to witness in the wretched wigwams of his own people and what he here saw in this bright little tent of Memotas. It was all so new and strange to him. Everybody seemed so happy. No rude words were spoken by the boy to his mother, and there was no tyrannising over his sister. With equal affection Memotas treated Meyockesik and Sagastao, and great was his kindness and attention to his wife. At first Oowikapun's old prejudices and defective education regarding women almost made him believe that Memotas was lacking in brave, manly qualities. Why should he thus allow his wife and daughter to be on such terms of equality with himself and his son? But when he became better acquainted with him he found that this was not the case.

Oowikapun could not then solve this question; neither did he until in after years. Then the solution came to him as it had come to Memotas.

There was one custom observed in the wigwam of Memotas that gave Oowikapun more surprise than any of these to which we have referred, for it was something which he had never heard or seen before. In the morning and evening Memotas would take out of a bag a little book printed in strange characters, and read from it, while his wife and children reverently and quietly sat around him and listened to the strange words. Then they

would sing, in a manner so different from the wild, droning,
monotonous songs of the conjurers, that Oowikapun was filled
with a strange feeling of awe, which was much increased when
they all knelt down reverently on the ground, and Memotas
seemed to talk with the Great Spirit, and really called Him
his Father. Then he thanked Him for all their blessings,
asked His forgiveness for everything they had done that was
wrong, and asked His blessing upon his family and everybody else—even upon his enemies. And then, before he ended,
he besought the Good Spirit to bless Oowikapun, and not only
heal his wounds, but take the darkness from his mind and
make him His child. And he always ended his prayers by
asking the Good Spirit to do all these things for the sake of
His Son, Jesus.

All this was very strange and even startling to Oowikapun.
He had lived all his life in a land dark with superstition and
paganism. The gospel had as yet never been there proclaimed.
The name of Jesus had never been heard in that wild north land.
As none of the blessedness of religion had entered into the hearts
of the people, so none of its sweet, loving, elevating influences
had begun to ennoble and bless their lives and improve their
habits. He pondered over what he witnessed and heard. He
was thankful when the day's hunting was over. Memotas would
talk to him as they sat there on their robes around the fire, often
for hours at a time. From him he learned how it was that they
had so changed in many of their ways. Memotas told him of
the coming to Norway House of the first missionary, the Rev.
James Evans, with the book of heaven, the words of the Good
Spirit to His children. He told him many of the wonderful
things it speaks about, and that it showed how man was to love
and worship God, and thus secure His blessing and favour. The
little book which Memotas had was composed of the four gospels
only. These Mr. Evans had had printed at the village himself
in Indian letters which he had invented, and called syllabic
characters. They are so easily learned by the Indians that in
a few weeks those who were diligent in their studies were able
to read, very fluently, those portions of the Word of God already

translated for them, as well as a number of beautiful hymns, some of which he had heard them sing. Oowikapun had never heard of such things, and was so amazed and confounded that he could hardly believe that he was in his right mind. Memotas tried to give him some idea of the syllabic characters in which his little book was printed. He made little sentences with a piece of coal on birch bark, and then handed them to his wife or children, who easily read out what had been written. That birch bark could talk, as he expressed it, was a mystery indeed.

When the time came for Oowikapun to return to his home Memotas went with him quite a distance. He had become very much interested in him. Being a happy, converted Christian himself, he was anxious that this man, who had come to him and been benefited physically, should hear about his soul's need and the Great Physician who could heal all his diseases. Lovingly and faithfully he talked to him and urged him to accept of this great salvation. Then he asked him to kneel down with him, and there, out alone with him and God, Memotas prayed earnestly that this dark pagan brother might yet come into the light of the gospel. Then he kissed him, and they parted, not to meet again for years.

Happy would it have been for Oowikapun if he had responded to Memotas' entreaties, and even tried to become a Christian. But the heart is hard and blinded as well as deceitful, and the devil is cunning. So long, sad years passed by ere Oowikapun, after trying, as we shall see, other ways to find peace and soul comfort, humbled himself at the cross, and found peace in believing on the Lord Jesus Christ.

Oowikapun returned to his little lodge, rekindled the fire, and tried to enter upon his hunting life where he had left off when wounded by the wolf. He stretched the furs already secured, then, early next morning, visited his traps, and spent the rest of the day hunting for deer. His success was not very great. The fact is, what he had heard and witnessed during the days of his sojourn in the wigwam of Memotas had given him so much food for thought that he was not concentrating his mind on his work in a manner that would bring the greatest success. He would sometimes get into a reverie so absorbing that he would stop in the trail and strive to think over and over again what he had heard about the good Book and its teachings. Very suddenly one day he was roused out of one of these reveries. He had gone out to visit some traps which he had set in a place where he had noticed the tracks of wild-cats. While going along through a dense forest, with his gun strapped on his back, he got so lost in thought that his naturally shrewd instincts as a hunter, sharpened by practice, seemed to have deserted him, and he nearly stumbled over a huge old she-bear and a couple of cubs. With a growl of rage at being thus disturbed, the fierce brute rushed at him, quickly broke up his reverie, and brought him back to a sense of present danger. To unstrap his gun in time for its successful use was impossible; but the ever-ready sharp-pointed knife was available. Accustomed to such battles, although never taken before so unexpectedly, Oowikapun sprang back to the nearest tree, which, fortunately for him, was near at hand. With a large tree at his back, and a good knife in his hand, an experienced Indian has the advantage on his side, and can generally kill his savage antagonist without receiving a wound. But, if attacked by a black bear in the open plain, armed with only a knife, the hunter rarely kills his enemy without receiving a fearful hug or some dangerous wounds.

One of the first bits of advice which an experienced Indian hunter gives to a young hunter who goes out anxious to kill a bear, or who may possibly, while hunting for some other game, be attacked by one, is to get his back up against a tree so large that if the bear is not killed by the bullet of his gun, he may be in the best possible position to fight him with his knife. It is no child's play. A wounded, maddened bear is a fierce foe. The black bear's method of attacking his human antagonist is quite different from that of the grizzly bear of the Rocky Mountain region. The grizzly strikes out with its dreadful claws with such force that he can tear a man to pieces, and is able to crush down a horse under his powerful blows. But the black bear tries to get the hunter in his long, strong, arm-like fore legs and then crush him to death. The hug of a bear, as some hunters know to their cost, is a warm embrace. Some, who, by the quick, skilful use of their knives, or by the prompt arrival of a rescue party, have been rescued from the almost deadly hug, have told me how their ribs have been broken and their breast-bones almost crushed in by the terrible hug. I know of several who have been in such conflicts, and although they managed to escape death by driving their knives into some vital spot, yet they had suffered so much from broken ribs and other injuries received that they were never as strong and vigorous afterwards. But with a good tree at his back, his trusty knife in his hand, and his brain cool, the advantage is all on the side of the hunter.

Among the many stories told of such conflicts, there is one by a Canadian Indian, which shows that even the women know how to successfully conquer in these encounters. This hunter was out looking for game, and had succeeded in killing a deer, which he left in the woods for his wife to skin, while he returned to his wigwam for his sled on which to drag it home. It was in the spring of the year, and there was still snow on the ground. A great, hungry bear that had just left his den after his long winter's sleep, while prowling about looking for food, got on the scent of the blood of the newly-killed deer. Following it up, he soon reached the spot where the Indian woman was skinning the animal. She had just time to spring up with the knife in her hand, and back up against a tree close at hand, ere the half-famished brute sprang on the deer and began devouring it. Seeing the woman so close, he seemed to think it best to get rid of her before eating his meat, and so, with a growl, he rushed at her. He raised himself up on his hind-legs, and tried to get his fore-paws around her and thus crush her to death. She was a brave woman, and knew what to do. Holding the knife firmly in her hand, she waited until his hot breath was in her face and he was trying to crowd his paws in between her back and the tree against which she was pressing herself with all her might. Then, with all her force, she plunged the sharp-pointed knife into his body in the region of his heart, and gave it a quick, sharp turn. So thoroughly did she do her work that the great, fierce brute could only throw up his paws and fall over dead. The brave squaw had killed him without receiving a scratch herself. When the husband returned with the sled, he found that not only had his wife skinned the deer, but also a big black bear.

CHAPTER III.

His victory.—The cubs captured.—Starts for home.—Visits the village of pagan relatives.—Urged to join in the wild dance of propitiation to the devil.—Memories of Memotas at first restrain him.—Yields at last.—Dances until he falls unconscious.—Left alone in a bark wigwam.—His sad condition.—His wonderful dream.

"ON HIS JOURNEY TO HIS FAR-AWAY NORTHERN HOME."

CHAPTER III.

OOWIKAPUN was taken off his guard for once. But he was soon himself again. Before the infuriated beast could get her paws around him, one quick, vigorous thrust of his knife, and his antagonist, armed only with teeth and claws, lay dead before him. So sudden had been the attack, and so quick had come the deliverance, that for the first time in his life Oowikapun offered up, as well as he could, words of thanksgiving to the Great Spirit for his escape. In his own crude way, and with the Indian's naturally religious instinct and traditions, he had believed in the existence of a good spirit which he called Kissa Maneto. He also believed in a bad spirit, whose name was Muche Maneto. But in the worship he had engaged in heretofore he had endeavoured to propitiate and turn away the malice of the evil spirit, rather than to worship the good spirit, about whom he had had but very vague ideas until his visit to the Christian hunter's wigwam. Now, however, even before he skinned the bear, he prayed to that good Spirit, the giver of all his blessings, and was grateful for his deliverance. Would that he had continued trying to pray.

He was very glad to get the meat and skin of the bear, and also the two little cubs, which he easily captured alive. Bending down some small trees, he tied the greater portion of the meat in the tops, and then let them swing up again, as he could not carry much back with him in addition to the two frisky little bears. This plan of *cacheing* supplies in the tops of small trees, as the Indians call it, is almost the only way that things can be safely left in the woods where so many wild animals are prowling about. If the meat were put up in the branches of a large tree, the wolverines or wild cats would soon get on the scent of it, and, being able to climb the trees, would make short work of it. If buried in the ground, these animals would soon get it. But buried in the tops of the small trees it is perfectly safe. The animals cannot climb, and they have not wit enough to cut the tree down with their teeth. So the *cache* is safe until the owner comes for it.

Thus Oowikapun hunted until the season was almost ended. Then making a long, light sled he packed on it his furs, camping outfit, and the two young bears, which had become quite tame, and started out on his journey to his far-away northern home. Loaded as he was, he saw it would take him several days to make the journey, and so he resolved to go a little out of his way and visit a village of Indians at the meeting-place of three rivers. They were of the same tribe as his own people, and some of them were distant relatives. Unfortunately for him, they were in the midst of one of their superstitious dances. The dances and sacrifices of dogs were a kind of propitiatory offering to the Muche Maneto, the devil, to put him in good humour, so that he would not interfere with them and prevent their having great success in the coming spring hunt. Of course Oowikapun was invited to join in the dance. Much to their surprise he at first refused. This they could not understand, as in previous visits he had been eager to spring into the magic circle and display his agility and powers of endurance. When questioned as to his reasons for declining, he told them of his visit to the camp of Memotas, and what he had heard and witnessed. They gathered around him, and, Indian-like, listened in silence until he had told them his story. It was not only received with a good deal of incredulity, but with scorn. The men were astounded, and indignantly exclaimed,—

" So he lets his wife eat with him, does he? cuts the wood himself, carries the water, and prays to the Kissa Maneto to bless his enemies, instead of trying to poison or shoot them—that is the white man's religion, is it, which Memotas has accepted? Well, let him keep it. It is not what we want. As our fathers lived and died, so will we. And don't be a fool, Oowikapun. You will be wanting one of our daughters one of these days to be your wife ; then, if you treat her like Memotas treats his, she will be coming back and telling our women all about it, and there will be a pretty fuss. Oh no, this will never do. You have had bad medicine thrown into your eyes and you do not see straight."

Thus they answered him, and day after day bantered him. The poor fellow was anxious to follow the entreaties of Memotas, but as yet unconscious of the divine power which he might have had if he had only asked for it, and so, lacking the strength to resist these temptations of his heathen friends, especially when he heard from the lying conjurers that even the black-eyed maidens were talking about his strange unwillingness to join in the religious ceremonies, he yielded and sprang into the circle. Madly and recklessly he danced to the monotonous drummings of the old conjurers and medicine men, who had been fearful that they were about to lose their grip upon him. A wild frenzy seemed to have entered into him, and he danced on and on until even his hardened, stalwart frame could stand it no longer. Suddenly he fell upon the ground in a state of unconsciousness, and had to be carried to a little wigwam, where on a bed of spruce branches he was left to recover consciousness when he might.

Such occurrences among the Indians in their wild state, when celebrating some of their religious ceremonies, such as this devil worship or their sun or ghost dances, were not at all uncommon. Wrought up to a state of frenzy, some of these devotees ceased not their wild dancings day or night. They danced sometimes for three days continuously. Then, utterly exhausted, they fell into a deathly swoon, which often continued for many hours. In this sad plight was poor Oowikapun.

For hours he remained like a corpse. He was in a state of absolute unconsciousness, and without an apparent movement of either muscle or limb. After a time the mind began to act, and strange, distorted dreams and visions flitted through his disordered brain. At first all was confusion and discord. Then there came to him something more like a vision than a dream, and so vividly was it impressed upon him that it was never forgotten.

Here it is as told years after: Oowikapun dreamed that he was one of a large company of his people who were on a long journey which all had to take. It led them over high mountains and trackless plains, along swift rivers, and across stormy lakes, through great forests where fierce wild beasts were ever ready to spring upon them, and where quaking bogs were in the way to swallow up those who were for a moment off their guard. The company was constantly diminishing as they journeyed on, for the dangers were so many that death in various forms was constantly cutting them off. The survivors, full of sadness and hurried on by some irresistible impulse, could not stop long in the way. All they could do was to give those who had fallen a hasty burial, and then join in the onward march. Darker and darker became the sky, and worse and worse seemed the way. Still on and on they were impelled. They had to cross the wide, stormy lakes, and in every one of them some of the party were lost. In every rough portage some fell fainting by the way, and sank down to rise no more. The crouching panther and the fierce wolves in the dense forest were ever on the alert, and many a man and woman, and even some of the little children, fell victims to these savage beasts. A feeling of sadness and despair seemed to take possession of all. Vainly they called upon the conjurers and medicine men to get help from their Manetos to make the way easier, and to find some information for them why they were travelling on this trail, and the place to which it led. Very unsatisfactory were the answers which they received. They had no information to give about the trail. But they reported that they had heard from their forefathers that there was a place called the "happy hunting grounds" beyond the high mountains. But the way was long and dark, and they had no guide to lead them in the gloom, and none to tell them how they could find the passes

in the mountains. While thus almost broken-hearted in the
way, the thought came to Oowikapun, in his dream or vision,
that surely there must be a better trail than this rough one,
wherein so many of the people were perishing. With this thought
in his mind he resolved, if possible, to break away from the
company and try to find a safer path. If he failed in his efforts
and perished miserably in his search, what did it matter? They
were dying off very rapidly where they were, and things could
not be worse.

Then, if he succeeded in finding a better road where the skies
were bright, where storms came not, where portages were short
and easily passed, and the breezes on the lakes only wafted them
on their way,—if he could find a trail where no savage beasts
lurked, and could talk with some one who had been over the
way, or could tell him that it ended well,—if he could only
succeed in getting his people in this better path, how rejoiced he
and they would be.

Then it seemed in his dream that he made the effort to break
away. But he told no one of what was in his heart, or of his
resolves, for he was afraid of being ridiculed by his comrades
if he should try and then fail in his efforts. He found it very
hard at first to get out from the old trail, but he persevered and
succeeded.

He found the way become smoother, and in some way which
he could not understand help was being given him several times
just when he needed it. Cheering words and sweet songs at
times fell upon his ears, and made him forget that he was alone
and footsore in this trying work. Once, when his way led him
over a great lake, and he was out upon it alone in a little boat,
in which it seemed impossible for him to reach the farther shore,
and he was about giving up in despair, there came a strong,
firm hand upon the little helm, and soon he was safe at his
landing-place.

From this place the travelling was very much easier, and he
journeyed on, ever looking for the safer trail for his people.
Seeing before him a pleasant hill he hurried to its summit,
and there before him in the valley, stretching away in the

3

distance, on and on until lost in a golden cloud of brightness, like the sunlight on the waters, he saw a broad trail, smooth and beautiful, with a great company of happy people walking in it. As he watched more carefully he observed that some were Indians, and some were white people, and some of other colours. But all seemed so happy and bright and joyous, that Oowikapun wept as he thought of the unhappy condition of his own people in the other trail.

Wearied by his long journey, and charmed by the sight before him, he tarried there for hours, and then he thought he fell asleep, and while in this condition a man with a covered face came to him and gently aroused him, and, seeing that he had been weeping, asked in gentle, sympathetic tones why he should weep while before him there was so much joy and happiness.

Touched by the kindly manner of the stranger, Oowikapun forgot his usual reserve and told him all that was in his heart. While he talked the visitor listened in silence until he had told his sad story. Then, heaving a sigh that seemed full of sorrow, he said,—

"Has not the Great Spirit pitied you and tried to help you? Did He not send you to the wigwam of one of His followers to give you some directions about getting in the better way? Is He not waiting and watching to see how you are using what knowledge you have secured? Why have you so soon forgotten your first lesson?"

Then he quickly moved to go. As he turned away, the covering for an instant dropped from his face. Oowikapun got a glimpse of it, and it vividly reminded him of Memotas.

CHAPTER IV.

"THE DEERSKIN DOOR OF HIS LODGE WAS PARTIALLY BUT NOISELESSLY PULLED ASIDE.

CHAPTER IV.

WITH a start Oowikapun awoke from his long sleep, confused and bewildered. So vivid had been his dream that it was some time before he could grasp his surroundings and come back to life's realities.

It was a night of intense darkness. Fierce, cold winds came shrieking out of the dense forest and shook the little bark tent into which he had been thrown. No cheerful fire burned in the centre, and there was not a person in the wigwam to offer aid or help. Every bone and muscle in his body seemed to ache, and his mind was so distracted and his nerves unstrung that he was thoroughly miserable. He was nearly destitute of clothing, for he had been carried out from the circle just as he had danced and fallen, and now here he was nearly naked and shivering with the cold. Vainly he groped about for his fire-bag in which he carried his flint and steel that he might strike a light; but in the inky darkness nothing could be found. Only a visitor in the village, he felt, with Indian reserve, that it would be a great breach of decorum and a sign of great weakness if he were to call for help. So in spite of his aches and shiverings he resolved that he would at least be a "brave," and patiently endure until the morning brought him light and friends.

Very long, indeed, to Oowikapun seemed that cold, dark night. The reaction had come, and physically and mentally he was to be pitied. His dance had carried him very near to the verge of the dance of death. And then in reference to his vivid dream, although as yet he could not interpret much of it, still there was the vague idea, as a haunting fear, that it had come to him to chide him for his cowardice in falling back and taking part in the devil dance after having heard of the other way. Filled with sorrow he sat on his rude bed of boughs, hour after hour, with his locked hands clasping his knees, and his head bowed upon his breast.

The few sounds which broke the stillness of those hours or interrupted the sighing of the winds were not pleasant. A great owl, ensconced in a tree not far away, maintained for a long time its monotonous "hoot-a-hoot a-hoo," while away in the distant forest gloom, rising at times shrill and distinct above the fitful wind, he heard the wail of the catamount, or panther, the saddest and most mournful sound that ever broke the silence of forest gloom. It is a sound so like the wail of a child in mortal agony that, heard close at hand, it has caused the face of many a brave wife of the backwoods settler to blanch with terror and to cry out with fear. Its despairing wail seemed to poor Oowikapun as the echo of the feeling of his saddened heart.

But the longest night has an end, and to the patient watchers day dawn comes again. So it was in this case. As the first rays of light began to enter in through the cracks and crevices of the wigwam, Oowikapun rejoiced greatly, and then fell into a heavy sleep.

When he awoke the camp fire was burning brightly on the ground before him, a warm blanket was over his shoulders, and food, warm and inviting, near the fire, was ready for him.

Oowikapun rubbed his eyes, rose up and shook himself, and wondered whether this was a vision or a reality. His keen appetite, sharpened by long fasting, came to his help, and naturally aided in the settling of the question. So he vigorously attacked the food, and was soon refreshed and comforted.

Just as he was about finishing his meal the deerskin door of his lodge was partially but noiselessly pulled aside, and his outer garments and Indian finery, including his prized fire-bag, all of which he had thrown off at the beginning of the dance, were quickly placed inside the door. The thing was done so speedily and quietly that it nearly escaped his notice, sharp and quick as he was. A draught of air coming in through the partly opened door caused him to turn and look, but he was only in time to see a hand and a shapely arm, on which was a beautifully wrought bracelet of Indian bead-work, draw close again the curtain-like door.

It would have been considered a great breach of decorum if he had manifested any curiosity or had arisen to see who the person was to whom he was indebted for this kindness. So curbing all curiosity he finished his breakfast and put on his apparel. Strange to say, he seemed anxious to be as presentable as possible. Then going out he was soon greeted by his friends, who all began urging him to accept of their hospitalities and eat with them. When Oowikapun stated that he had eaten already a hearty meal they were all amazed, and doubly so when he told them of what had been done for him in the wigwam while he slept. Their heartless custom had ever been to leave the unconscious dancer alone and uncared for until he emerged from the tent, and then offer him their hospitality. But here had been a strange innovation, and the question was immediately raised, Who has done this? In spite of many enquiries everybody seemed to be in ignorance.

Oowikapun's curiosity was now aroused, and he became exceedingly desirous to find out who this benefactor was. He wanted to express his gratitude. Among other plans that were suggested to his mind was to endeavour to find out who had taken charge of his clothing and fire-bag while he was dancing in the tent. But even here he failed to get any clue. Everybody seemed to have become so absorbed in the ceremonies of the dance, or in watching the endurance of the dancers, that all such minor things were forgotten. When the conjurers and medicine men came to congratulate Oowikapun on his efforts, and called his dances "good medicine," a sudden feeling of abhorrence and repulsion came into his heart toward them. As quickly as he dared he turned from them in disgust, and resolved to get out of the village and away from their influence as soon as possible.

His few preparations were soon completed, and saying "What-

cheer," the Indian farewell, he securely fastened his little bears
with his furs upon his sled, and throwing the strap over his
shoulder, he resumed the trail that led to his still distant home.
Soon he was out of the village and in the forest. Snares and
traps abounded on each side of the path, for the game was plentiful. Especially were the rabbits and white partridges, the
beautiful ptarmigan, very abundant that winter and spring, and
hundreds were caught in snares by the boys and women and girls.
For a time he had the well-beaten trail over which these people
travelled as they daily visited their snares.

On pushed Oowikapun until nearly every snow-shoe track of
these hunters had disappeared. The sense of being alone again
in the forest, or nearly so, returned to him with depressing results.
Rapidly and vividly did there pass through his memory the events
of the last few days. Especially did his singular dream come up
before him. A feeling of remorse filled his heart that he had
yielded to the importunities of his pagan friends and had been
persuaded to take any part in the dance. Then his thoughts
went farther back, and he was with Memotas again, and the
memory of their last walk came up distinctly. Especially did
he remember the loving words about the true way. Then as
he recalled the spot where with him he bowed in prayer,
and put up his hand on his brow where the good man's
kiss had been imprinted, the very spot seemed to burn, and
Oowikapun could have wept, only for his indignation at his
cowardice.

Thus moodily he strode along on the trail, now nearly destitute
of all evidences of travel, when he was startled and amazed by a
strange sound.

It was a woman's voice he heard. And although the tones
were low and plaintive, yet he could easily make out the words
of the song. He had heard them over and over again in the
wigwam of Memotas. They were:

> " Jesus net it a ye-moo-win,
> Is pe-mek ka ke it oo-tate,
> We-ya pi-ko ne mah-me-sin,
> Nesta a-we itoo ta-yan."

To our readers who may not be posted in the Cree language of
the far north we give the English translation of the verse:

> " Jesus my all to heaven is gone,
> He whom I fix my hopes upon ;
> His track I see, and I'll pursue
> The narrow way till Him I view."

This hymn, one verse of which we give, was the first one
translated into the Cree. It is a universal favourite, and is
frequently heard, not only in the public religious services and at
the family devotions, but often the forest stillness is broken by its
cheering notes. Mr. Evans printed in syllabic characters his first
copies of it on birch bark, as he had no paper.

But how did it get out here so far away in the wilderness?
And who was the sweet singer? These were questions now in
the mind of Oowikapun as he stood still in the trail, uncertain
what to do, but strangely thrilled by the song, which had so
quickly carried him back to the tent of the loving Christian
Memotas.

CHAPTER V.

The beautiful singer.—The sudden meeting in the narrow trail.—The tell-tale bracelet.—The candid conversation.—Our heroine's past history.—One year she had heard of Jesus.—Had known Memotas, and James Evans.—Now was persecuted by her pagan relatives.—Sang her sweet song in the forest solitudes.—" Astumastao," our heroine.

"HAVE I NOT SEEN THAT BEAUTIFUL BRACELET BEFORE?"

CHAPTER V.

NOT long had he to wait, for soon there emerged from among the young balsam trees a fair Indian maiden. She carried a number of snow-white ptarmigan and a few rabbits which had rewarded her skill as a huntress, as well as her enterprise in coming so far from the village to set her snares. She was taller than are most Indian maidens, and her eyes were bright and fearless. As she stepped into the trail and turned her face homewards, she gave a sudden start as, lifting up her eyes, she found herself face to face with Oowikapun. Quickly regaining her composure, she threw her game over her back, in the Indian woman's style of carrying her loads, and, with the natural Indian womanly modesty, seemed anxious to at once go on. It appeared probable that not a word would have passed between them. However, just at the moment when the maiden swung her load of game on her back, the shawl she was wearing fell back for an instant from her arm, and on it Oowikapun's quick eye detected the beautiful bracelet that he had seen that morning on the arm that had closed the door of his little lodge.

This discovery filled him with curiosity, and he resolved to find out who she was, and why she had shown him, a stranger, so much kindness. But the difficulty was how to begin. His natural Indian training told him it would be a breach of decorum to speak to her, but so great was his anxiety to find the solution of what even was a mystery to the villagers themselves, that he felt he must not let the opportunity pass by. Man's bluntness is his own poor substitute for woman's superior tact, and so, as she was about to pass, he said, " Have I not seen that beautiful bracelet before ? " He tried to speak kindly, but he was excited and fearful that she would be gone. So his voice sounded harsh and stern, and it startled her. Her face flushed a little, but she quickly regained her composure, and then quietly said, —

" It was made years ago ; so you may have seen it before."

" Was it not on the arm of the friend who made the fire and prepared the food and brought the clothing for the poor, foolish stranger ? " he answered.

She raised her piercing black eyes to his, and, as though she would look into his soul, she said, without hesitancy, —

" Yes, it was ; and Oowikapun was indeed foolish, if not worse."

Startled and confounded at this reply, given in such decided tones, Oowikapun, in spite of all his efforts to appear unmoved, felt abashed before her, and his eyes fell under her searching gaze.

Recovering himself as well as he could, he said, " Will the fair maiden please tell me what she means ? "

" Yes," she answered : " what she means is that she is very much surprised that a man who for days has been a guest in the wigwam of Memotas and Meyoo-achimoowin, and who has heard their songs and prayers to the Good Spirit, should again be found in the circle of the devil dance."

" How do you know I was with Memotas ? " he replied.

" From your own lips," she answered. " I was with the maidens, with only a deerskin partition dividing us from the place where you told the men of your battle with the wolf, and of Memotas' words about the book of heaven and the Good Spirit to you. And yet," she added, and there was a tinge of sorrow in her voice, " after having heard that you went to the old, bad way again."

Stung by her words, so full of reproof, he retorted with some bitterness, " And you and the other maidens goaded me on to the dance."

With flashing eyes she drew herself up proudly, and said, "Never! I would have died first. It was a lie of the conjurers if they said anything of the kind."

A feeling of admiration, followed by one of almost envy, came over him as he listened to the decided words uttered with such spirit, and he heartily wished some of it had been his when tempted to join in the dance of sin. With the consciousness of weakness, and with his proud spirit quelled, he said: "Why are you of this mind? How is it that you know so much about the white man's way? Did I not see you in the wigwam of Kistay-imoowin, the chief whose brother is the great medicine man of the tribe? How is it that you, the chief's daughter and the conjurer's niece, should have such different thoughts about these things?"

Her answer, which was a little bit of her family history, was as follows :—

"While I am the niece of Koosapatum, the conjurer and medicine man, whom I hate, I am not the daughter, but the niece, of Kistayimoowin, the chief. My father was another brother of theirs. He was a great hunter, and, years ago, when I was a little child, he left the home of his tribe, and, taking my mother and me, he went far away to Lake Athabasca, where he was told there was abundance of game and fish. In a great storm they were both drowned. I was left a poor orphan, about six years of age, among the pagan Indians, who cared but little for me. They said they had enough to do in looking after their own children, so I often was half-starved. Fortunately for me the great missionary, with his wonderful canoe of tin, which the people called the 'Island of Light,' came along that way on one of his great journeys. He had those skilful canoe-men, Henry Budd and Hasselton. While stopping among the people and teaching them the true way, the missionary heard of me and of the danger I was in of perishing, and so they took me in the canoe and carried me all the way to Norway House. It was long ago, but well do I remember how they carried me across the rough portages when I got tired out, and gave me to eat the best pieces of ducks and geese or other game which they shot

for food.   At night they gathered old hay from the beavers'
meadows, or cut down a young balsam tree, and with its branches
made me a little bed for the night.   When we reached Norway
House Mission I was adopted into the family of the missionary.
They and Miss Adams, the teacher, were very kind to me.   I
joined the Indian children in the school, and went regularly to
the little church.   I well remember Memotas and Big Tom, and
Mustagon and Papanekis, and many others.   I learned some of
the hymns, and can distinctly remember seeing the missionary and
Mr. Steinheur printing the hymns in the characters on the bark and
paper.   It was the happiest year of my life.   Oh that I had been
wise, and tried to gather up and fix in my memory all that was
said to me of the Great Spirit and His Son Jesus, and about the
good way !   But I was a happy, thoughtless little girl, and more
fond of play with the little Indian girls and the fun-loving,
happy boys than of listening to the teacher and learning my
lessons.

"A year after my Uncle Kistayimoowin came down to the
fort with his furs and took me away home with him, and here,
so far away, I have lived ever since.   In his way he is not
unkind to me, but my Uncle Koosapatum hates me because I
know these things ; and, as all are in dread of his poisons, even
Kistayimoowin does not wish me to speak about what I heard
that year, or sing what I remember, except when I am far out in
the forest.   Because I do not want to have my uncle, the chief,
poisoned I keep quiet sometimes, but most of the women have
heard all I know, and they are longing to hear more.   So our
hearts got full of hoping when, as we waited on the chief with
his dinner a few days ago, and we heard him talking with some
others who were eating with him, that you had come and had
been cured of your wounds by a Christian Indian by the name
of Memotas, and were going to give a talk about what had
happened to you and you had heard.   When I heard him
mention the name of Memotas, I thought I would have dropped
the birch roggin of roasted bear's paws which I was holding at
the time ; for I could still remember that good man so well.
Gladly I gathered some of the women together behind the

partition to listen and learn more of the good way, if we could, from you.

"We drank in every word you said, and when they mocked we were very angry at them, but we dare not say a word for fear of a fearful beating. While you stood firm and refused to join in that wicked dance, we rejoiced. When you yielded, our hearts became sad, and we silently got away. I went out into the woods and wept. When I returned, the women had shut themselves up in their tents, and the men were all off to the big dance-house. I found your clothes and fire-bag just where you had thrown them off, in danger of being dragged away or torn to pieces by the foolish young dogs. So, unseen by anybody, I gathered them up and put them away.

"During the days and nights you danced I was angry and miserable, and at times could not keep from weeping that a man who had known Memotas, and for days had been with him, and had heard so much about the good way, should then go back to the old, dark way which gives no comfort to any one. When you fell senseless in the circle, I watched where they carried you. I visited the tent in the night, and I heard your sad moans, and I knew you were unhappy. At daybreak, as you had fallen into a deep sleep, I built the fire and prepared the food and carried you your clothing; and if it had not been for the breeze through the door when I last opened it you would never have known anything about me."

Her story very much interested Oowikapun. As he listened to her talking, as he had never heard an Indian woman speak before, he saw the benefit which had come as the result of a year spent among Christians, even if it were only a year in childhood. When she finished, he said : "I am glad I have met you and heard your story."

"Why should you be glad?" she replied. "I am sure you must have been offended that a woman should have dared to speak so plainly to you."

"I deserve all you have said, and more too," he added, after a pause.

"In which trail are you in the future going to walk?" she asked.

4

This straight, searching question brought vividly before his vision the dream and the two ways which there he saw, and he felt that a crisis in his life had come; and he said, after a pause,—

"I should like to walk in the way marked out by the book of heaven."

"And so would I," she replied, with intense earnestness. "But it seems hard to do so, placed as I am. You think me brave here thus to reprove you, but I am a coward in the village. I have called it love for my uncle's life that has kept me back from defying the conjurers and telling everybody I want to. But it is cowardice, and I am ashamed of myself. And then I know so little. Oh that we had a missionary among us, with the book of heaven, as they have at Norway House and elsewhere, that we might learn more about the way, and be brave and courageous all the time!"

This despairing cry is the voice of millions dissatisfied with the devil dances and worship of idols. The call is for those who can tell them where soul-comfort can be found, and a sweet assurance brought into their hearts that they are in the right way.

Hardly knowing what answer to make, but now interested in the woman as never in one before, he asked,—

"What name does your uncle call you?"

Wishing to find out her name, he put it in this way, as it is considered the height of rudeness to ask a person his name. When several persons are together, and the name of one is desired by one of the company, the plan is always to ask some third party for the desired information.

"Astumastao," she replied. And then, feeling with her keen, womanly instincts that the time had come when the long interview should end, she quickly threw her game, which had been dropped on the ground, over her shoulder again, and, gliding by him, soon disappeared in the forest trail.

CHAPTER VI.

Oowikapun still on the trail.—Troubled with many conflicting thoughts.—
Disgusted with paganism and yet in the dark as to the way to the
Cross.—Increased activity as a hunter.—The goose hunt.—His wise
words at the council fires.

"HE REFUSED THE PROFFERED MEAL AND EVEN THE LIGHTED PIPE."

CHAPTER VI.

TO Oowikapun this interview was of great value; and while he could not but feel a certain amount of humiliation at the cowardice he had been forced to confess or admit, and felt also that it was a new experience to be thus talked to by a woman; yet his conscience told him that she was right, and he deserved the reproofs she had given; and so, with something more to think about, he resumed his onward journey, and when he stopped that night and made his little camp he was many miles nearer his home.

As he sat there by his cheery fire, while all around him stretched the great wild forest, he tried to think over some of the new and strange adventures through which he had passed. With startling vividness they came before him; and above all the brave words of the maiden, Astumastao, seemed to ring in his ears. Then the consciousness that he who had been trying to make himself and others believe that he was so brave was really so cowardly took hold of him, and so depressed him that he could only sit with bowed head and burdened heart, and say within himself that he was very weak and foolish, and all seemed very dark.

The stars shone out in that brilliant northern sky, and the aurora danced and blazed and scintillated; meteors flashed across the heavens with wondrous brightness, but Oowikapun saw them not. The problem of life here and hereafter had come to him as

never before. He had found out that he had a soul, and that
there was a God to fear and love, who cared for men and women ;
and that there was reward for right doing and punishment for
sin. So with the little light he had, he pondered and thought ;
and the more he did the worse he got, for he had not yet found
the way of simple faith and trust. And so he became so saddened
and terrified that there was but little sleep that night for him,
and as there he sat, longing for help, he remembered the words
of Astumastao : " Oh that we had a missionary among us, with
the book of heaven, that we might learn more of the way, and be
brave and courageous all the time."

So in this frame of mind he watched and waited until the first
blush of morn ; then after a hasty meal, prepared on his camp-
fire, he started off, and in due time reached his home in the distant
village in the wilderness ; and in the depressed mood in which we
here first met him, he lived for many a day.

The change in him was noticed by all, and many conjectured
as to the cause. But Oowikapun unburdened not his heart, for
he knew there were none among his people who could understand ;
and with bitter memories of the cowardice at the village of his
relatives, he thought in his blindness that the better way to
escape ridicule, and even persecution, would be to keep all he had
learned about the Good Spirit and the book of heaven locked up
in his heart.

Oowikapun was one of the best hunters in his village, and as
his father was dead and he the oldest son (now about twenty-five
years of age) he was looked up to as the head of the wigwam.

In his Indian way he was neither unkind to his mother nor
to the younger members of the family. To' his little brothers he
gave the two young bears, and they soon taught them a number
of tricks. They quickly learned the use of their forelegs, and it
was very amusing to see them wrestling with and throwing the
young Indian dogs, with whom they soon became great friends.

Oowikapun, to divert attention from himself, and to keep from
being questioned about the change in his conduct which was so
evident to all, devoted himself with unflagging energy to the
chase. Spring having now opened, the wild geese came in great

flocks from their southern homes to those northern lands, looking
for the rich feeding grounds and safe places where they could
hatch out their young. These times when the geese are flying
over are as a general thing very profitable to the hunters. I
have known an old Indian with only two old flint-lock guns in
one day kill seventy-five large grey geese. That was, however,
an exceptional case. The hunters considered themselves fortunate
if each night they returned with from seven to twelve of these
birds.

Oowikapun having selected a spot at the edge of a great marsh
from which the snow had melted, and where the goose grass was
abundant, and where the flocks were flying over in great numbers,
hastily prepared what the hunters call their nest. This is made
out of marsh hay and branches of trees, and is really what its
name implies—a nest so large that at least a couple of men can
hide themselves in it. When ready to begin goose-hunting they
put on a white coat and a cap of similar colour, for these observant Indians have learned that if they are dressed in white
they can call the geese much nearer to them than if their
garments are of any other hue. Another requisite for a successful hunt is to have a number of decoy geese carved out of wood
and placed in the grass near the nest, as though busily engaged
in eating.

Oowikapun's first day at the hunt was fortunately a very good
one. The sun was shining brightly, and, aided by a southern
breeze, many flocks of geese came in sight in their usual way of
flying, either in straight lines or in triangles. Oowikapun was
gifted in the ability to imitate their call, and so he succeeded in
bringing so many of them in range of his gun that ere the day
ended he had bagged almost a score.

In after years when I visited that land it used to interest me
very much, and added a pleasurable excitement to my trip, to
don a white garment over my winter clothing, for the weather
was still cold, and join one of these clever hunters in his little
nest and take my chance at a shot at these noble birds. I felt
quite proud of my powers when I brought down my first grey
goose, even if I did only break a wing with my ball.

Quickly unloosing Cuffy, one of my favourite Newfoundland dogs, I sent her after the bird, which had lit down on a great ice field about five hundred yards away. But although disabled, the bird could still fight, and so when my spirited dog tried to close in upon her and seize her by the neck, the brave goose gave her such a blow over the head with the uninjured wing that it turned her completely over, and made her howl with pain and vexation. Thus witnessing the discomfiture of my dog, I could easily understand what I had been frequently told by the Indians of foxes having been killed by the old geese when trying to capture young goslings from the flocks.

In these annual goose-hunts all the Indians who can handle a gun take part. The news of the arrival of the first goose fills a whole village with excitement, and nothing can keep the people from rushing off to the different points, which they each claim year after year, where they hastily build their nests and set their decoys.

I well remember how quickly I was deserted by a whole company of Saulteaux Indians, one spring, on their hearing the long-expected call of a solitary goose that came flying along on the south wind. I had succeeded, after a good deal of persuasion, in getting them to work with me in cutting down trees and preparing the soil for seed-sowing, when in the midst of our toil, at about ten o'clock in the forenoon, the distant "Aunk! aunk! aunk!" of an old grey goose was heard, the out-skirmisher of the oncoming crowds. Such was the effect of that sound upon my good hunters, but poor farmers, that the axes and hoes were hastily dropped, and, with a rush, they were all off to their wigwams for their guns and ammunition, and I did not see them again for a month.

Success in the goose-hunt seems to elate the Indian more than in anything else. Why, I could never find out. It may be because it is the first spring hunting after the long dreary winter, and there is the natural gladness that the pleasant spring time has come again. Whatever it may be, I noticed for years more noisy mirth and earnest congratulations on success in the goose hunt than in anything else.

Loaded down with his game, Oowikapun returned to his wigwam, and instead of cheerily responding to the congratulations of the inmates on account of his success, he threw himself down on his bed, silent and gloomy, and refused the proffered meal and even the lighted pipe which his mother brought him.

Surprised were they all at his conduct, which was so contrary to his old ways. He had never been known to act like this before—just the reverse. He had come to be considered the brightest young man in the village. He had more than once been called the young hunter of the cheery voice and the laughing eyes. Then, in his serious hours, in times when the affairs of the tribe were being discussed, at the council fires, so good was his judgment, and wise and thoughtful, even beyond his years, were his words considered, that even the old men, who seldom did anything else but sneer at the words of the young men, gave respectful attention to what fell from the lips of Oowikapun. Well was it remembered how that only last year, at the great council fire of the whole tribe, when the runners brought the news of the aggressions of the whites on some of the southern tribes with whom they had been, in years past, in friendly alliance, and the old men spake with bitterness and talked of the old glories of the red men ere the pale-face came with his fire-arms, and what was worse, with his fire-water, and hunted down and poisoned many of their forefathers, and drove back the rest of them toward the setting sun, or northward to the regions of the bitter cold and frost; and how much better it would have been, they said, if their forefathers had listened to the fiery eloquence and burning words of Tecumseh and his great brother, the prophet, and joined in a great Indian confederacy, when they were numerous and strong, to drive the white man back into the sea,—then it was, when eyes flashed, and the Indians were wild enough with excitement to cause great trouble, that Oowikapun arose and spoke kindly words. They were also wise beyond his years.

CHAPTER VII.

His words were all for peace with the pale-face. Now he is unhappy.—
Many conjectures.—Afraid to pray, he seeks advice from the old man
of the village.—His terrible story of the wicked white fur-traders, and
their fire-water.— How the old man was robbed, and his wife insulted.
—Her flight through the forest, and return home.—Mookoomis tells the
Indian tradition of the origin of the human race, and why all men are
not of the same colour.—And why the white man has obtained the
mastery.

"'THEY ONLY LAUGHED AT MY QUESTION.'"

CHAPTER VII.

IN his address he urged that the time for successful war was passed; that Tecumseh himself fell before the power of the pale-face; that his wampum and magic pipe had disappeared, and his tomahawk had been buried in a peace ceremony between his survivors and the paleface; and, bitter as might be some of the memories of the past, yet to all it must be clear that, as many of the white men were really their friends, it was for their interest and happiness to act patiently and honourably toward them, and strive to live as the Great Spirit would have them—as loving brothers.

Thus talked Oowikapun last year. Why is it, they said, that he, who gave such promise of being a great orator as well as a successful hunter, should act so strangely now? Some said he was losing his reason and becoming crazy. The young folks said he was in love with some bright-eyed maiden, whom they knew not; but many of the dark-eyed maidens hoped she was the fortunate one. And so they wondered why he did not let it be known. As he still delayed they said it is because he has had so many to support that he is poor, and is fearful that what he has to offer in payment for his bride might not be considered sufficient, and he would be humiliated to be refused.

Even some of the older women, not born in beauty's hand-basket, when they could get away from their exacting husbands, would sit down under the bank where the canoes were drawn up, and

gravely, in imitation of the men around their council fires, would
exchange opinions, and, like white folks, gossip a little in reference
to conduct so extraordinary.

The old conjurers and medicine men were at length consulted.
They said, after long drumming and pow-wowing, and the consum-
ing of much tea and tobacco at the expense of his relatives, that
the spirits of the forests and rivers were calling to him to fast and
suffer and prepare to become a great medicine man; and that
nature would then reveal her secrets and give him power and
influence over the people and make him Good Medicine if he
obeyed her voice.

Oowikapun heard of the surmisings and mutterings of the
people about him, and at first was very much annoyed.   Then, no
peace coming to him, for he was afraid to pray to the Good Spirit
since he had taken part in the devil dance, he decided to consult
one of the old men of the village who had a reputation among the
people as being well posted in old Indian traditions and legends.
The young man was cordially welcomed to the wigwam of the old
man.   But Oowikapun had not been there very long in conversation with him before he found out that he was a great hater of
the whites.   On Oowikapun expressing some surprise at this, and
asking his reason for having such bitterness in his breast toward
the pale-faces, the old man told him a strange story.

He said that one winter, many years ago, when he was a great
hunter, he had been very successful in the chase and had caught
quite a number of black and silver foxes, as well as many otters
and other valuable fur-bearing animals.   Thinking he could do
better in selling his furs by going down the rivers and across many
portages far away to a place where he had heard that white men
had come who wished to trade with the Indians, and who had sent
word that they would give a good price for rich furs, he set off for
that place.   He took his wife along with him to help paddle his
canoe and to carry the loads across the portages, which were very
many.   They reached the place after many days' journey.   The
white men, when they saw their bales of rich furs, seemed very
friendly, and remarked that as they had come so far they must be
very weary.   They gave him their fire-water to drink and told him

that it would make him forget that his hands were sore with long paddling his canoe, and that his feet were weary with hard walking in the portages. So, because they professed to be his friends, he drank their fire-water and found out that they were his enemies. They gave him more and more, telling him it was good, and he foolishly drank and drank until he lost all of his senses, and was in a drunken stupor for days.

When he came to himself he found he was out in a cold shed and very miserable. His head ached and he was very sore. His coat was gone and so were his beautifully beaded leggings and moccasins. His gun was also gone, and with it his bales of rich and valuable furs. His wife was also gone, and there he was, half-naked and alone.

Alarmed, he cried out, and asked how it was that he was in such a sad plight. Hearing him calling out, some of those white men who had pretended to be his friends came to him, and said,—

"Begone, you poor Indian fool!"

"Where are my furs?" he asked.

With a laugh, they said,—

"We have taken them for the whisky you drank."

"Give me my furs," he cried, "or pay me for them."

"But," added the old man, "they were stronger than I, and had taken away not only my gun, but my axe and knife, and so I was helpless before them.

"'Where is my wife?' I then asked. But they only laughed at my questions, and it was weeks before I heard that they had insulted her and would have foully treated her but that she had pulled out her knife and threatened to kill the first man that touched her. While keeping them away with her knife she moved around until she got near an open window, when she suddenly sprang out and fled like a frightened deer to the forest. After long weeks of hardship she reached the far-off home. She . had had a sad time of it and many strange adventures. Foot-sore and nearly worn out she had been at times, but she bravely persevered. Her food had been roots and an occasional rabbit or partridge which she snared. Several times she had been chased by wild animals. Once for several days the savage wolves madly howled around the foot of a tree into which she had managed to climb for safety from their fierce attacks. Fortunately for her a great moose deer dashed along not far away, and the wolves which had been keeping watch upon her rushed off on its trail. Hurrying down she quickly sped on her way. Thus had she travelled all alone, her life often in jeopardy from savage beasts. But she feared them less than she did the rude white men from whom she had fled."

The man, when kicked out of the place of the white traders, had, after a couple of days' wanderings, fallen in with some friendly Indians, who took pity on him, clothed and fed him, and sent him back in care of·some of their best canoe men. He thus reached home long before his brave wife did, who had to work her way along as we have described.

Oowikapun listened to the story of the old man with patience until he closed. Then in strong language he expressed his horror and indignation. It was very unfortunate that he should have heard it in the state of mind in which he was at that time. From his meeting with Memotas and Astumastao, he had inferred that all white men were good people, but here was a rude awakening from that illusion. Terrible, indeed, have been the evils wrought by the white men in these regions where dwell the red men. The native prejudices, and even their superstitious religions, are not as great hindrances to the spread of the gospel among them as are the abominable actions and rascalities of white men who bring in their fire-water and their sins from Christian lands.

For a time the old man Mookoomis exerted quite a strong influence over Oowikapun, and many were the hours they spent together. Oowikapun was in that state of restlessness that the only times he could be said to be at peace were when either engaged in the excitements of hunting or when listening to Mookoomis' excited words as he talked away hour after hour of the old legends and traditions of his people, whose glory, alas, was now about departed.

One evening, when a few interested listeners were gathered around the wigwam fire of the old story-teller, and they had made him happy by the gifts of venison and tobacco, Oowikapun said to him, —

"Good father, you are wise in many things about which we are ignorant, and long ago the old men of our people handed down to you from our forefathers the stories to be kept in remembrance; tell us how the white men came to be here. If you know we should like to hear also of the black people of whom the runners from other tribes have told us, who also exist in great numbers."

All joined in this request. So when the old man had filled and smoked his calumet again, he told them the Indian tradition of the origin of the human races. He said,—

"Long ago, perhaps as many moons as there are stars in the sky, the Great Spirit made this world of ours and fitted it up as a dwelling-place for his people. Then he set to work to make man. He took a piece of white clay and moulded it and worked at it until he had formed a man. Then he put him into an oven which he had prepared, and there he baked him to make him firm and strong. When he took him out of the oven he found that he had kept him in too long and he was burnt black. At this the Great Spirit was not pleased, and he said, 'You will never do,' and he gave him a great kick which sent him away south to that land where they have no snow, and where it is very hot, and told the black man that that was to be his land.

"Then the Great Spirit took another piece of clay and moulded it out and formed another man and put him in the oven to bake. But as he had burnt the first one so badly he did not leave this second one in long enough. When he took him out he found that he was still very white, and at this he was not pleased, and he said, 'Ugh! You will never do. You are too white. You will show the dirt too easily.' So he gave him a great kick which sent him across the sea to the land where the white man first came from to this country.

"Then," said Mookoomis, "the Great Spirit tried again. He gathered the finest clay he could find and moulded it and worked with it until he was well pleased with it. Then he put it into the oven to bake it; and now, having the wisdom which came from the experience of the other two failures, he kept this one

5

in just the right time. When he took him out he was of a
rich red colour. He was very much pleased, and said, ' Ho, ho !
you just right; you stay here.' So he gave this country to the
Indian."

This origin of the human race, which differs so considerably
from that of Mr. Darwin, very much interested Oowikapun and
his companions, and they urged Mookoomis to tell them from
Indian traditions how it was that the races had gotten into the
conditions that they now are. When the old man had filled and
smoked his pipe again and had seemed to be lost in thought for a
time, he began again :

"When the Great Spirit had made these different men and
given each wives of their own colour, he went away to his dwell-
ing place beyond the setting sun, and there abode. After a while
he thought he would come back and see how the men were getting
on. So he called them to meet him at a certain place, and as he
talked with them he found they were unhappy because they had
nothing to do. When the Great Spirit heard this he told them to
come back to-morrow, and he would make this all right for them.
On the morrow when they had met they saw that the Great
Spirit had three parcels. He laid them on the ground and told
them they were to choose which they would have. As the parcels
differed very much in size it was decided that they would cast
lots and thus settle who should have the first choice. When this
was done it was found that the black man was to choose first, the
red man second, and the white man would have to take what was
left. So the black man chose the largest parcel, and when he
opened it he found that it contained axes and hoes and spades
and shovels and other implements of toil. The Indian selected the
next largest bundle, and when he opened it he found that it contained bows and arrows and spears and lances and knives and
other weapons used by the hunter. Then the turn of the white
man came, and he took up the last parcel, which was a small
one, and when he had opened it there was nothing in it but a
book.

"When the black man and the red man saw that the white
man had nothing but a book they laughed out loudly and ridiculed

him very much. But the Great Spirit reproved them, and said, 'Wait a while and perhaps you will think differently.' And so they now do, for it has come to pass that because of the possession of that book, the white man has become so learned and wise that he is now much stronger than the others, and seems able to make himself master of the other races, and to take possession of all lands."

CHAPTER VIII.

Mookoomis' sad advice to unhappy Oowikapun.—His attempts to find peace for his soul in communion with Nature.—All sad failures.—God in Nature without Christ ever a mystery.—He looked for peace, and found everything was just the reverse.—The beautiful fawn killed by the fierce wolf.—The strife among the birds.—Cruelty and death everywhere.—The coming thunderstorm arouses his hopes for some answer of peace, even in her power and grandeur.—Oowikapun thrown helpless and stunned to the ground, while his wigwam is completely shattered.—One more attempt.—The wonderful auroras.—A most glorious display.—The corona of dazzling splendour.—The blood-red crimson terrifies, alarms, and crushes him into the dust.—Something more than Nature's phenomena necessary to lead to Christ.

"IT CRUSHED DOWN THE LITTLE WIGWAM INTO A HOPELESS WRECK."

CHAPTER VIII.

OOWIKAPUN heard Mookoomis tell these weird old stories at the camp-fires, and in listening to him he tried to forget his own sorrows and anxieties.

When he thought he had become so well acquainted with Mookoomis that he could make a confidant of him, he told him a little of what he had learned from Memotas; but he was careful to hide his own secret feelings. He knew Mookoomis was a strong pagan as well as a great hater of the whites. Not having met with any of the detested race who were Christians, he thought they were all alike, and believed they had only come across the ocean to rob and cheat and kill the poor Indian and take possession of all his lands.

One evening when they were alone Oowikapun ventured to tell him about the book of heaven which the white man had, and which some Indians had got hold of and were reading with great interest, and that some of them had even accepted its teachings. This news made Mookoomis very angry. Oowikapun was sorry that he had told him, but it was now too late, and so he had to listen while the angry man talked and gave his views on these things. He said that the Great Spirit never intended the book for the Indian, but that he had made him a hunter and sent him out into the forests and prairies, and on the great lakes and rivers, and where he was to listen and hear the Great Spirit's voice and see his works. "This," said Mookoomis, "is the Great Spirit's plan, and he will be angry with any of his red children who become dissatisfied with this arrangement and try to go the white man's way or read his book."

These talks did not bring comfort to Oowikapun or lift the burden from his soul. In his desperation he told Mookoomis of his heart sorrows and disquietude of spirit. The old man did not get angry, but listened to him very patiently, and then advised him to go out into the woods, away from every human sound, and in her peaceful solitudes let nature speak to him and soothe his troubled spirit.

So Oowikapun obeyed the voice of Mookoomis, and, quickly arranging his affairs, went out into the solitudes, far away from any human beings. He hoped that while there alone with nature he might get rest for his soul. In doing this he was only imitating thousands who, too stubborn or too ignorant to come to the Great Comforter in His own way, are trying in some other way to find that peace which God alone can give. We pity those who ignorantly do these things, but what can we say of those who have been taught the plan of salvation through faith in the Lord Jesus Christ, and yet will go on talking pertly about God in nature, and of their ability to find themselves in Him by studying Him in His works? God in nature without Christ is a riddle, a perplexity, a mystery.

We pity poor Oowikapun. Just enough light had come to him to show him that he was a poor miserable sinner, but he had not yet received enough to reveal to him the true plan of salvation. He is still groping along in the gloom, and is much more to be pitied than the thousands who know in theory what God's plan of salvation is, but who reject it because of their pride or hardness of heart.

Everything seemed against him. His eyes were opened to see things now as never before. Not as a skilful hunter, but as a seeker after peace was he out in nature's solitudes. Everything around him seemed mysterious and contradictory. This teacher, nature, whose lessons he had come to learn, seemed to be in a very perverse mood, as if to impart just the reverse of what he would learn, and seemed to be destitute of the very things he had hoped she would have imparted to him.

Sharp and rude was his first awakening from his illusion. He had not gone very far into the wilderness before it came to him, and it happened in this way : As he was walking along in the forest he heard a short distance ahead of him a pitiful cry of a creature in distress. He hurried on, and was just in time to see the convulsive gasp of a beautiful young fawn that had been seized and mangled by a fierce wolf, which had found it where it had been hidden away by the mother deer before she had gone out into the beaver meadows to feed.

To send the death-dealing bullet through the brain of the savage wolf was the work of an instant, but, alas ! it was too late to save the innocent little fawn, whose great, beautiful eyes were already glassy in death, and whose life-blood, pouring out from the gaping wounds, was crimsoning the leaves and flowers where it had fallen.

" Is this," said Oowikapun, with sadness of spirit, " the first lesson nature has for me ? To her I am coming for peace and quietness of spirit, and is this what I first see ? "

Thus he travelled on until he reached the shores of a great lake. Here he had resolved to stay for a time, at the advice of Mookoomis, to try to find, in the solitudes, the communion with nature for which his soul craved. A student of nature he had ever been, but never before with such an object in his heart as now filled it. But he found no happiness in his investigations, and was appalled at the sights which met him and the mysteries which sprang up upon every side. Death and discord seemed to reign everywhere, and the strong seemed ever ready to oppress the weak.

Such sights as the following were ever before him : One day while sitting near the shore of the lake, where the sunlit waters played with the pebbles at his feet, he saw a beautiful kingfisher. It hovered in mid-air for an instant, and then suddenly plunged down in the water, rising quickly again with a fine fish in his bill. On the top of a dead tree near the shore a fierce hawk had seen the fish captured, and, with a scream that rang out sharp and clear, it flew swiftly after the kingfisher, and so terrified it that it dropped the fish and hurriedly flew away to a place of safety. Seizing the fish in its bill with a scream of triumph, the hawk was about to return to the shore, when another actor appeared upon the scene. Away up on the side of the cliff, which rose up a little back from the shore to the height of several hundred feet, on a projecting ledge of rocks, a pair of eagles came year after year and built their crude, wild nest. One of these great birds was watching the battle below. When it heard the shrill scream of triumph from the fishhawk, it knew that the time for action had arrived. Like a thunder-bolt, with both wings closed it shot down from the eyrie, and before the hawk with its stolen plunder had reached its old storm-beaten tree, the king of birds struck it a blow that dazed and terrified it, and, dropping the fish, it barely succeeded in getting away. It was not the fishhawk the eagle was after, but the fish. As the active bird saw the fish drop from the beak of the fishhawk, it flew down after it and caught it in mid-air, and then, in majestic circles, it slowly ascended to its eyrie. This sight, under other circumstances, would have been enjoyable to Oowikapun, but now, when he was a seeker in nature for peace and happiness, the greed and rapacity of the stronger over the weaker only filled him with sadness.

Thus for several weeks he closely studied nature, and tried hard to learn lessons from her, while, far away from all his people, he dwelt in a little camp which he had made at the foot of a beautiful birch tree. But he was no better off, for all the sights that met his eyes were very similar to those we have described. It was cruelty and death and destruction everywhere.

Nature unaided does not reveal Christ the Saviour. Since the entrance of sin, with all its attendant miseries, into this once glorious world, the study of nature with all her vagaries, without the light of revelation to clear up her mysteries, is more apt to drive men away from God than to draw them to Him.

So Oowikapun found out especially one night while tossing about on his bed of balsam boughs. Lying there utterly miserable and dissatisfied with himself, he was startled by the far-away dull, sullen roar of thunder, which told of an approaching storm. Such was his mood that this sound was welcomed, and he sprang up rejoicing. There had suddenly come into his mind the thought that perhaps now he would hear something in nature's voice from which he could draw comfort and happiness.

With this hope in his heart he went out of his tent and seated himself on a rock near at hand. One by one the stars disappeared as the thick black clouds came rolling up, covering the whole expanse of heaven and making the night one of inky darkness, save when the cliffs and forest, islands and lake, were illuminated by the vivid lightning's flash. Soothed by that awesome feeling which comes to many in the brief last moments which precede the burst of the tempest, Oowikapun was comforted, and began to say to himself: "At last I hear the voice of nature for which I have so long been waiting, and now, so tranquillized, I wait for all she has to tell me 'of comfort and of rest.'"

Hardly had these thoughts passed through his mind before there came a lightning flash so vivid and a thunderbolt so near and powerful, followed by a crashing peal of thunder so sudden and so deafening, that Oowikapun was completely stunned, and thrown helpless to the ground. When he recovered consciousness the storm had nearly died away. A few muttering growls of thunder could still be heard, and some flashes of lightning upon the distant horizon told in which direction the storm had disappeared. Oowikapun staggered to his feet and tried to comprehend what had happened. That something had struck him was evident. What it was at first he was too bewildered to understand. Thinking the best thing he could do in this dazed condition would be to go back under the shelter of his tent, he turned to do so, but this he found an impossibility. The thunderbolt that had so stunned him had struck that large birch tree and shattered it. As it fell it had crushed down the little wigwam into a hopeless wreck.

Great indeed was the disappointment and vexation of Oowikapun. While vainly imagining that at length he was about to hear the soothing voice of nature to comfort and bless him, he had received from her such a crack that he was knocked senseless, and, in addition, had his dwelling-place completely wrecked.

Groping around in the ruins, he succeeded in finding his blanket, which he threw over his shoulders as a slight protection against the heavy rain which continued falling all night.

Oowikapun still lingered in his lonely forest retreat. His pride revolted at the idea of having to return to the village and confess that all his efforts had been in vain, and that only defeat and humiliation had been his lot.

So a new wigwam was built in a more sheltered place, amidst the dark evergreen trees. His depression of spirit was such that for a long time he only left his abode when hunger compelled him to hunt for his necessary food. When he did resume his wanderings they were generally in the night. The singing of the birds had no charm for him, and the brightness of the summer days chased not away his gloom. More congenial to him were the " watches of the night," when the few sounds that fell upon his ears were weird and ghostly. Here amidst the gloomy shadows, where the only sounds were the sighing of the winds among the trees, the melancholy hootings of the owls, or the distant howlings of the wolves, he passed many weary hours.

The Psalmist with adoring love could say, " Day unto day uttereth speech, and night unto night showeth knowledge," but to Oowikapun neither the " speech " of the day nor the " knowledge " of the night gave any responsive answer to his heart's longings, or led him any nearer to the source of soul comfort. And yet nature spake to him as grandly as it was possible for her to utter her voice, and her last effort was of the sublimest character, and such as but few mortals are permitted to witness.

It came to Oowikapun one night when he had aimlessly wandered far out from the shadows of the forest gloom, to a spot where the canopy of heaven, bright with its multitudes of stars, was above him. Perhaps in no other land can nature in her varied aspects of sublimity and grandeur, as regards celestial phenomena, be better studied than in the wild northland. Her cyclonic storms in summer, and her blizzard blasts in winter, are at times not only terrific in their destructive power, but they are also overwhelmingly grand in their appearance.

Then her "visions of the night" are at times sublimely beautiful. Her star-decked vault of heaven, absolutely free from all mists and fogs and damps, seems so high and vast. The stars glisten and twinkle with wondrous clearness. The flashing meteors fade out but slowly, and the moon is so white and bright that her shadows cast are often as vivid as those of the sun in some other lands.

But nothing equals a first-class field night of the mysterious Aurora Borealis. No other phenomenon of nature in magnitude of display, in varied brilliancy of colour, in bewildering rapidity of movement, in grandeur so celestial, in its very existence so unaccountable, is calculated to lift man up, and away from things earthly, into the very realm and presence of the spiritual, as does a first-class display of the northern lights, as seen in the far northland.

While they are generally more frequent in the winter months than at other times of the year, yet they are very uncertain in their coming, and sometimes burst upon the world and illuminate and fill up with celestial glory the brief hours of some of the short summer nights.

To Oowikapun, in his mental darkness and disquietude, there came one of these more than earthly visions of entrancing beauty.

If in any one of nature's phenomena she could speak to a troubled soul, surely it would be in this. For while to Elijah the answer was in the "still small voice," yet man, unaided by Divine revelation, prefers the earthquake and the fire, or some other grand overwhelming manifestations of nature's power, which appeals to the sensuous rather than to the spiritual. To these northern Indians the auroras have ever been associated with the ghostly or spiritual. In some of the tribes the literal translation of the northern lights is, "the spirits of their fore-fathers going out to battle."

The display that Oowikapun gazed upon was one of more than ordinary sublimity. He had left his little wigwam, which nestled among the balsams, and had gone out from the forest gloom, and had seated himself on the shore of the lake where the little waves made soothing music as they played among the pebbles at his feet. The sun had gone down in splendour, leaving a glorious radiance of sapphire and crimson on hills and waves. Quietly and imperceptibly the shadows of night mantled the long twilight gloaming, and then one by one the stars came out from their hiding-places, until the whole high dome of heaven was bright with their sparkling light. The Milky Way brightened into wondrous distinctness, until it seemed, to Oowikapun, like a great pathway, and he wondered, as held in the tradition of his people, if on it, by-and-by, he should travel to the happy hunting grounds of his fathers. After a time a brightness began to dawn in the northern sky, and then from it some brilliant streams of light suddenly shot up to the heavens above. Then many ribbons of light quickly followed, and, rapidly unrolling themselves parallel with the horizon, quivered and danced in rhythmic movements, blazing out at times in varied vivid colours, as they gracefully undulated from east to west. Often had Oowikapun seen these displays, but up to this time he had only gazed with languid interest upon these nightly visitants.

This night, however, there was a display so glorious that he stood as one entranced. With a suddenness that can only be shown by electrical phenomena, there almost instantaneously shot up from below the eastern horizon a dazzling blaze of gorgeous electrical light, which in successive bounds rushed on and on, until, like a brilliant meteor, a million times magnified, it spanned the heavens, and for a time, in purest white, it seemed to hang an arch of truce from heaven to earth. For a little while it quivered in its dazzling whiteness, and then from it flashed out streamers in all the colours of the rainbow. With one end holding on to the arch of snowy whiteness, they danced and scintillated and blazed until the whole heavens seemed aglow. Then breaking loose, they seemed to form themselves into whole battalions of soldiers, and advanced and fought and retreated, until the heavens seemed to be the battle-field of the ages, and stained with the blood of millions slain. During all the apparent carnage great streamers waved continuously above the contending armies, and seemed like great battle-flags leading on the forces to greater deeds of valour. Sometimes they seemed to change into great fiery swords, ready to add to the apparent carnage and destruction that seemed so intensely real.

Thus in ever changing glories the vision of the heavens above continued, while Oowikapun, awed and subdued in spirit, felt thankful that he was only a spectator upon such scenes of ghostly carnage and blood.

But impressive an l glorious as was what had already been revealed, the auroras had yet in reserve the climax of their display, and when it came it nearly froze his blood in his veins, and threw him trembling and terrified upon his face upon the ground. Suddenly did the change come. With the rapidity of a lightning flash the great quivering arch of light transformed itself into a corona of such dazzling splendour that no words can describe it. From purest white, the multitudes of streamers, of which it was now composed, suddenly changed to pink and blue and green and yellow, all the time flitting and scintillating so rapidly that the eyes were pained in their vain efforts to follow their rapid flights. Then, in the twinkling of an eye, the whole changed to a deep blood-red crimson—so blood-like, so terrible, so dazzling, so awful, that the brave man was crushed down, terrified and subdued, before this blinding display of the omnipotent power of the Great Spirit.

The dauntless courage that had made him exult at the prospect of meeting the fiercest bear in the forest with no other weapon than his trusty hunting knife, or the most hostile foe of his tribe, was of no avail here, and so, a crushed and vanquished man, as soon as he could he cowered back to his wigwam, where, wrapping himself in his blanket, he long remained. He trembled at the thought of having been in such apparent contact with the spirit-land, while his unhappy soul chided him with a sense of his unfitness for that unknown life beyond.

Poor Oowikapun! He was like many who, although they live under happier influences, and amidst the blaze of gospel-day, yet foolishly think that if some heavenly manifestation of the glory beyond, some glimpse of the land that is afar off, or some sight of its celestial inhabitants, were given them to enjoy, very quickly would they be convinced and converted.

John, the beloved disciple, saw the New Jerusalem and its inhabitants. Dazzled, overwhelmed, and confused he fell at the feet of one of those redeemed ones, and worshipped the creature instead of the Creator.

Something more than the mere visions of heaven's glories or northern auroras is necessary to give peace to the troubled soul. Even so found unhappy Oowikapun, for when the excitement of these night visions wore off, he felt more than ever crushed down with a sense of his own littleness, while darker seemed his spiritual vision than even before these auroral glories had blazed and flashed around him.

Disgusted and disappointed, he packed up his few things and returned to his village, more miserable and depressed in spirit than ever.

He had had many evidences of a Creator, but had met with nothing that told him of a Saviour. The idea of being able to " look up through nature unto nature's God " is an utter impossibility, unless the one looking has some knowledge of God in Christ Jesus. With this knowledge in his possession he can answer as did the devout philosopher who, when asked the question, " What are the latest discoveries in nature ? " replied, " God everywhere."

With God revealed in Christ Jesus there is something real in which to trust. Then mysteries that long perplexed are cleared up, and darkness that long continued is dissipated; and the trusting child realises that no longer is he slowly and feebly feeling his way along on the " sinking sands " of uncertainties, but is built on the " Rock of Ages."

CHAPTER IX.

Oowikapun confesses his complete failure to find peace for his troubled spirit in Nature.—Mookoomis' dreadful advice.—To try the trial of torture.—Hock-e-a-yum.—The journey to the Far West.—The terrible ordeal.—The agony and sufferings, all in vain.—No voice of comfort, no peace, no pardon.—Return home.—Society shunned.—A sudden resolve.—Determined to go and see Astumastao, the brave girl who knew something of the right way.—Something about her.—Free as a prairie breeze.

"LEFT HIM TO STRUGGLE AND PULL," ETC.

CHAPTER IX.

SHORTLY after his return to the village Oowikapun found his way to the tent of Mookoomis, and candidly told him of his complete failure to find comfort or peace of mind in communion with nature. He said he had faithfully carried out his directions, but that everything that he had hoped would have in it help or satisfaction seemed to have had just the reverse. Mookoomis listened intently to all he had to say; then, perhaps for the first time in his life, freely admitted his own dissatisfaction and uncertainty of belief in their Indian way. But he was an obstinate, wicked old man, and determined, if possible, to keep Oowikapun walking, as he again said, " as our forefathers walked." So he urged him to make the great trial of fasting and personal torture, and see if in the delirium of physical agonies the voice of comfort for which he was longing would not come to him.

For a long time the young man hesitated to undertake this terrible ordeal. It is called by the western Indians the Hocke-a-yum, and is a ceremony so severe and dreadful that many an Indian has never recovered from its agonies.

Great indeed must be the wretched disquietude that will cause human beings, who naturally shrink from pain, to endure what thousands voluntarily submit to if only they can get peace to their souls.

Oowikapun spent weeks in a state of indecision, and then resolved to follow the advice of old Mookoomis. In his blindness and folly he found himself in company with a vast multitude, who in their ignorance and superstition are hoping by self-inflicted torture on their bodies to atone for sin and merit heaven.

Great indeed is this company of deluded ones. They are found by the missionaries almost everywhere.

The poor, ignorant Hindoo, on the burning plains of his native land, seated on a stone pillar, with arm extended until it has become fixed and rigid, while the growing finger-nails have pierced through his clenched hand, is one of the sad company. Another one is that poor fanatic who measures the whole distance of many hundreds of miles which stretches from his jungle home to the Ganges by prostrating his body on the ground as a measuring rod. In this sad procession are millions and millions of unhappy ones, without God, and therefore without hope.

Poor Oowikapun is now in this sad company. All his fears are aroused, and in his vain efforts to quiet them he is about to go through a most severe ordeal of fasting and acute physical suffering. How terrible is sin! How sad is the fall! How dreadful must be the goadings of the guilty conscience when men, and women too, will so punish themselves, hoping thereby they can find relief.

When the young Indian had finally resolved on his course of action he immediately set about carrying it out. He joined himself to a company of "braves" who were also going to pass through the ceremony of Hock-o-a-yum. Different motives were in the hearts of those who were about to undergo the trying ordeal. Some of them were ambitious to succeed as great warriors and as hunters. Others were ambitious to become leaders or great medicine men among the tribes. To succeed in their ambitious purposes it was necessary that the ordeal of suffering should be passed through.

While the majority were thus fired by their selfish hopes of attaining prominence and position as the result of their sufferings, there were several like Oowikapun who were unhappy in their souls and were going to try this method in the hope of relief. Perhaps, like him, they had been in some place where a few rays of light had shone upon their souls. These had revealed to them the sinfulness of their lives and the hideousness of sin, but, being ignorant of the Great physician, they were going to see if there was any efficacy in these trying ordeals.

As the ceremonies were only held in the Far West, where the devotees gathered from various tribes, Oowikapun and those with him had to travel for many days ere they reached the place.

Far beyond the limits of the hunting grounds of his people did he and his deluded comrades journey. They had to work up the swift current, and make many portages around the rapids of the Nelson River. Then across the northern part of treacherous Lake Winnipeg they ventured in their frail canoes, and only their consummate skill in the management of these frail boats saved them from going down to watery graves.

Up the mighty Saskatchewan for nearly a thousand miles they hurried on. If their minds had not been troubled at the prospect of their coming sufferings, they would, as hunters, have been delighted by that trip through that glorious western country, which then teemed with game. Multitudes of buffalo, coming down to the great river to drink, first gazed on them with curiosity, and then, when alarmed, went thundering over the plains. The great antlered elks were seen in troops upon the bluffs and hills, and bears of different kinds went lumbering along the shores. Beautiful antelopes, with their large luminous eyes, looked at them for a moment, and then went flying over the prairies like the gazelles in the desert.

They landed at Edmonton, where now there nestles in beauty on its picturesque bluffs a flourishing little town. Oowikapun and his comrades in those days, however, found only the old historic fort, even then famous as the scene of many an exciting event between the enterprising fur traders and the proud, warlike Indians of the plains.

Here they left their canoes, and after exchanging some furs for needed supplies, they started south-west on the long trail

of many days' toilsome travelling, until at length the place of
the fearful ordeal was reached.

Into all the details of the scenes and events of the Indian
ceremony of torture I am not going to enter. Catlin has with
pen and brush described it in a way to chill the blood and fill
our sleeping hours with horrid dreams. Suffice it to say that
Oowikapun at once put himself in the hands of the torturers.
First of all they kept him for four days and nights without
allowing him a mouthful of food or drink. Neither did they
permit him to have a moment's sleep. Then they stripped off
his upper garment, and cutting long parallel gashes in his breast
down to the bone, they lifted up the muscles and tied to the
quivering muscles ends of horse-hair ropes about three-quarters
of an inch in diameter. The other ends of these two ropes were
fastened to a high pole about fifteen feet from the ground.
At first the upper ends of the ropes were drawn through rude
pulleys, and poor Oowikapun was dragged up six or eight feet
from the ground, and held there for several minutes by the
bleeding, lacerated, and distended muscles of his breast. Then
the ropes were suddenly loosened from above, and he fell with
a sickening thud to the ground. Quickly they raised him up on
his feet and made fast the ropes to the upper end of the pole,
and left him to struggle and pull until the muscles rotted or
were torn away and he was free. Four days passed by ere he
succeeded in breaking away, and during that time not a morsel
of food or a drop of water was given him.

Weeks passed away ere Oowikapun recovered from those
fearful wounds. After all, what did they accomplish for him?
Nothing at all. He was, if possible, more wretched in mind
than in body. No voice of comfort had he heard. No dispelling
of the darkness. No lifting of the heavy load. No assurance
of pardon. No peace. Is it any wonder that he was about
discouraged, and that his sharp-eyed neighbours looked at him
at times and said one to another that something must be wrong
with him in his head?

To convince them that his mind was not disordered or his
reason affected, the young Indian attended the councils of the

tribe, and ever showed himself clear-headed in discussion and debate. He applied himself with renewed diligence to his work as a hunter, and remembering Memotas' love for his household, strove to imitate him in his conduct toward his mother and the younger members of his family.

Disgusted and annoyed that nothing but disappointment and suffering had come to him from following the advice of Mookoomis, he shunned his society and would have none of his counsel.

So passed the summer months. When the winter came again there arose in the heart of Oowikapun a peculiar desire to go and see Astumastao, the brave maiden who had been his real friend, and who had told him words which had done him more good than anything else he had heard since he had parted from Memotas. About her he had never spoken to any one. But her bright eyes had burned themselves into his heart, while her brave words had fixed themselves in his memory.

So making up some excuse about important business with his relatives in the distant village where dwelt the young girl, he prepared for the journey. He arrayed himself in new and picturesque apparel. With his little outfit packed on a light sled, his gun in his hand, and his axe and knife in his belt, he set off for the village where he had made such a sad fall after all his resolves to have nothing more to do with devil worship.

Visions of that former visit came fresh to his mind. All that had since transpired seemed like a horrid dream.

Is it thought surprising when we say that as he hurried along he forgot much of his sorrow and was filled with pleasurable excitement at the prospect of meeting Astumastao again? True, he would check himself and say that he was acting or thinking foolishly. Astumastao might be married, or the bride selected by her uncle for some one else, for all he knew. Why, then, should he think so constantly about her? True, she had been very kind to him in his sorrow; but then he had only met her once. Thus he reasoned with himself as he kept hurrying along, never trying very hard to banish her from his mind. And fortunate it was for Astumastao that Oowikapun was on the way.

When Astumastao returned to the village after her conversation with Oowikapun, she found the people excited by his story of the fire burning in his wigwam and the meal prepared and ready for him. How these things could have been done without any one finding it out when they are all so alert and quick-witted amazed them. Then it was to them such a breach of the rules or usage of such occasions. Who, they said in their excitement, could have been so presuming as to break the long established custom and take in food and fire to one of the dancers?

Some said one of their number must have done it while the others slept so soundly after the exciting days through which they had been passing. Others were tinged with superstition, and declared with bated breath that the gods must have had special love for him, and had themselves come and supplied his wants.

To all of these things Astumastao listened and, not being suspected, kept what she knew in her heart. She was an active, brave girl, and knew how to handle both the paddle and the gun. Kistayimoowin, her uncle, was pleased with her prowess and industry, and while possessing the pagan ideas about women, so that he would never allow himself to show them any particular affection, yet ever since she had been brought as a little child into his wigwam he had treated her not unkindly. With his superstitious nature he had been strongly influenced by the words of the missionary when he handed the orphan child over to his care, and had told him that if he wanted the favour of the Great Spirit he must treat her kindly and well.

And so it happened that as Kistayimoowin had no children of his own, this bright, active girl was always with himself and his wife as they, Indian like, moved from one hunting ground to another in quest of the different kinds of game. As she was so quick and observant, her uncle had taught her many things about the habits and instincts of the different animals, and the best methods known for their capture. The result was she had become a very Diana, skilful and enthusiastic in the chase.

Thus the years rolled on and she grew to beautiful young

womanhood. More than one pair of eyes looked toward her as the one they would like to woo and win, or, as they thought of it in their way of putting it, be able by abundant or valuable gifts to purchase her from her uncle. Up to this time, however, he had repelled most decidedly all advances made to him for her, and had acted in so harsh a manner toward all would-be suitors that they had been obliged to keep at a respectful distance. So Astumastao was still as free as a prairie breeze.

CHAPTER X.

"HE SUDDENLY ATTACKED THE CANOE."

CHAPTER X.

THE summer following the visit of Oowikapun, Kistayimoowin
had taken his wife and niece and gone out to an island in
one of the large lakes to hunt and fish. Theirs was the only
wigwam that summer on the island. While out in a small
canoe on the lake shooting ducks, one day his gun, which was
an old flint-lock, unfortunately burst. It not only wounded him
severely, but caused him to upset the canoe while out about half
a mile from the shore. His wife and Astumastao heard his wild
whoop of danger and quickly realised the sad position he was in.
Unfortunately, they had no other canoe, and no friendly helper
was within range of their voices. Astumastao, however, like all
Indian girls, could swim like a duck. So, without hesitancy,
she sprang into the lake and as rapidly as possible swam out
to the rescue of her wounded uncle, who so sorely needed her
assistance. The explosion of the gun had nearly blown off one
of his hands, and some pieces of the barrel had entered his body.
The result was he was very helpless and weak from the loss of
blood.

Astumastao reached him as soon as possible, and, finding it
impossible to right the canoe, resolved to try and swim with him
to the shore. It was a desperate undertaking. But she knew
just what to do to succeed. The wounded man could do nothing
to help himself, so she placed him where he could keep his un-

wounded hand upon her back, and thus keep afloat. Then she bravely struck out for the distant shore.

Only those who have tried to rescue a helpless person in the water can have any correct idea of the fearful task she had to perform. But, buoyed up by hope and her naturally brave heart, she persevered, and, although at times almost exhausted, she succeeded in reaching the shallow water, out into which her feeble aunt had ventured to assist her. As well as they could they helped or carried the almost exhausted man to the wigwam, and immediately made use of every means at their disposal to stop the wounds from which his life's blood was ebbing away.

The poor man was no sooner laid on his bed, weak and exhausted, than he turned his eyes toward Astumastao and startled her, although he spoke in a voice that was little above a whisper. What he said was :

"Nikumootah !"   [English, " Sing !"]

Astumastao hesitated not. Choking back her emotions, she began in sweet and soothing notes the song we have already heard her sing :

> "Jesus my all to heaven is gone,
> He whom I fix my hopes upon ;
> His path I see, and I'll pursue
> The narrow way till Him I view."

When she had sung two or three verses, the sick man said, -- "Who is this Jesus ?"

Not much was it that was remembered through all the long years that had passed away since Astumastao had received her last Sabbath-school lesson ; but she called up all she could, and in that which still clung to her memory was the matchless verse :

" For God so loved the world that He gave His only begotten Son, that whosoever believeth in Him should not perish, but have everlasting life."

The sick man was thrilled and startled, and said,—

" Say it again and again !"

So over and over again she repeated it.

"Can you remember anything more?" he whispered.

"Not much," she replied. "Only I remember that I was taught that this Jesus, the Son of the Great Spirit, said something like this, 'Him that cometh unto Me I will in no wise cast out.'"

"Did they say," asked the dying man, "that that included the Indian? May he, too, go in the white man's way?"

"Oh, yes," she answered; "I remember about that very well. The missionary was constantly telling us that the Great Spirit and His Son loved everybody, Indians as well as whites, and that we were all welcome to come to Him. Indeed, it must be so, for these are the words I have learned about it out of His great book : 'Him that cometh to Me I will in no wise cast out.'"

"Sing again to me," he said, and so she sang :

> "Lo, glad I come, and thou, blest Lamb,
> Shalt take me to Thee as I am.
> Nothing but sin have I to give,
> Nothing but love shall I receive."

"What did you say His name was?" said the dying man.

"Jesus," she sobbed.

"Lift up my head," he said to his weeping wife.

"Take hold of my hand, my niece," he said. "It is getting so dark, I cannot see the trail. I have no guide. What did you say was His name?"

"Jesus," again she sobbed. And, with that name on his lips, he was gone.

Call not this picture overdrawn. Hundreds of these Indians have long lost faith in paganism, and in their hours of peril, or in the presence of death, even those who have learned but little about Christianity cling to those who have some knowledge of the great salvation and strive to grope into the way.

The two women were alone on the island with their dead, and with no canoe by which they could return to the distant mainland. But Indian women are quick at devising plans to meet emergencies, and Astumastao speedily resolved on a scheme to bring help. What she did was this: she cut a long pole from a clump of slender trees which grew near their wigwam, and then, securely fastening her shawl to it, hoisted it up as a signal on a point where it was visible from the shore. Soon it was observed, and help came speedily.

There was a good deal of genuine sorrow expressed by the Indians in their own quiet way. After many questions had been asked and answered, they wrapped up the body in birch bark and conveyed it to the mainland, and there buried it with their usual Indian pagan rites, much to the regret of Astumastao.

Left alone with her aunt, who was quite feeble, upon Astumastao fell the chief work of supplying food for both. Bravely did she apply herself to the task, and such was her skill and industry that a good degree of success crowned her efforts. Very seldom, indeed, was their wigwam destitute of food. Often had she some to spare for the old and feeble ones, who, according to the heartless custom of some of the tribes when they reach the time of life when they can neither snare rabbits nor catch fish, are either thrown out of the wigwams in the bitter cold and left to freeze to death, or they are deserted in the forests and left to be devoured by the wild beasts.

When a poor orphan child, Astumastao had been rescued and kindly cared for, and she never forgot those early days and kindly deeds performed for her happiness.

During the remaining part of the summer which followed the sad death of her uncle, she succeeded in killing quite a number of reindeer, which are at times very numerous in those high latitudes. Annoyed by the numerous flies, these reindeer frequently rush into the great lakes and rivers, and, as the Indians can paddle their light canoe much faster than the animals can swim, they easily overtake and kill them.

Astumastao, with a couple of other Indian girls, succeeded in killing a number of them. Their plan was to lash a sharp knife to the end of a pole, and then, when they had paddled near enough, they stabbed the deer and dragged it ashore. All the deer do not give up without a struggle. This Astumastao found to her cost one day. She and a couple of young maidens about her own age had hurried out after a famous deer whose many-pronged antlers told that he was one of the great monarchs of the forest. When they tried to get near enough to stab him, he suddenly attacked the canoe with such fury that, although Astumastao succeeded in mortally wounding him, yet he so smashed it that it was rendered useless, and the girls had to spring out and swim to the shore, which was a long way off. However, they reached it in safety, amidst the laughter of the people, who had observed their discomfiture. Nothing daunted, however, the plucky girls quickly secured another canoe, paddled out, and brought in their splendid deer.

When the long, cold winter set in again, Astumastao applied herself very diligently to the work of trapping and snaring rabbits and some of the smaller fur-bearing animals. In her hunting excursions she followed her plans of the preceding winters, and often plunged farther into the dense forests to set her traps and snares beyond those of any other woman-hunter.

Here, in the solitude of nature, she could sing to her heart's content, while deftly weaving her snares or setting her traps. On one of these trips she caught a glimpse of a black fox, and, suspecting him to be the thief who had been robbing her snares of some rabbits during the last few days, she resolved, if possible, to capture the valuable animal. His rich and costly fur would buy for herself and aunt some valuable blankets and other things much required for their comfort. Returning quickly back to her wigwam, she succeeded in borrowing a fox-trap from a friendly hunter. Then, making all preparations, she started very early the next morning for the spot where she intended setting her trap. The distance was so great that she had to tramp along for several hours on her snow-shoes ere she reached the place. But the air was clear and bracing, and, hoping for success in her undertaking, she felt but little fatigue. Skilfully she set the trap, and then, walking backwards, with a heavy balsam branch she carefully brushed out her tracks. She retraced her steps to the ordinary trail, and began collecting her rabbits and partridges from the snares. Although the fox had robbed her of several, yet she was more than ordinarily successful, and gathered sufficient to make a heavy load.

At one place the path led her through a dense, gloomy part

7

of the forest, where the great branches of the trees seemed to interlock above her head and shut out the light and sunshine. But she knew no such thing as fear. Throwing her heavy load over her shoulders, and supporting it with the carrying strap from her forehead, she cheerily moved along, thinking how happy she would be if she captured that fox on the morrow. Suddenly the shriek of a wild beast rang in her ears, and she was instantaneously hurled on her face to the ground.

CHAPTER XI.

Oowikapun on the trail.—Discovers the tracks of the fierce catamount, or mountain-lion.—Detects it following up a snow-shoe trail.—His excitement and alertness.—The terrible spring.—The well-sent bullet.—The fortunate rescue.—Our hero and heroine, Oowikapun and Astumastao, face to face.—Their glad words of thankfulness at her escape.—The wounds dressed.—The meal in the forest.—The journey to the village.—Great excitement of the people.—Oowikapun a hero in the eyes of all.—His frequent visits to the tent of the aunt of Astumastao.—He hears much of the good Book and of the true way.—And still he lingers.

'THE BEAST RAISED HIS HEAD,' ETC.

CHAPTER XI.

WE left Oowikapun hurrying along on willing feet at the place in the forest where he had first observed the snow-shoe tracks of the hunters of the village he was approaching. Observing that the tracks were those of a woman, he could not help hoping that they were those of the fair maiden whom he had met very near that same spot two winters before. This hope filled him with pleasant anticipation ; so on and on he hurried.

As he strode swiftly but quietly along, an object caught his attention that filled him with excitement. Crouching down, and yet hurrying rapidly along in front of him, not three hundred yards away, was an enormous catamount. This was not a mere lynx, or wild cat, but one of those great, fierce brutes more allied to the mountain lion of the Rockies, or the panther of the western and northern part of this continent.

As Oowikapun watched the graceful, dangerous brute gliding along before him, the thought came into his mind that perhaps this was the very one whose wild, weird shrieks had sounded in his ears so dolefully as he shivered in the little wigwam of the village he was now approaching. Knowing the habits of these animals, he supposed this one, from its rapid, persistent, forward movements, and the absence of that alert watchfulness which they generally possess, was on the track of a deer.

Oowikapun dropped to the ground and carefully looked for the tracks of the game that the catamount was pursuing. But to his

surprise he could not discover the footprints of any animal. All
at once the truth flashed upon him. The fierce brute was on the
trail of the woman, and, maddened by hunger, was resolved to
attack her. As he hastened on he became more thoroughly convinced of this, as he observed how, like a great sleuthhound, it
glided along in the snow-shoe tracks before him. Quickly did
Oowikapun prepare for action. His trusty gun was loaded with
ball. His knife and axe were so fastened in his belt that they
were ready for instant use, if needed. The strap of his sled was
dropped from his shoulders, and thus disencumbered, with all a
hunter's excitement in such a position, he followed cautiously and
rapidly. Indian trails are very crooked; so it was that he only
now and then caught a glimpse of the bloodthirsty brute. But
when he did, he observed it was intent on its one purpose, as it
hardly turned its head to the right or the left, as it crouched or
bounded along. Soon, however, the trail led from the open forest,
where the trees were not clustered together very closely, into a
dense, gloomy place of venerable old trees, whose great limbs
stretched and interwined with each other for quite a distance.
This was the same gloomy part of the forest into which we had
seen Astumastao go as she was returning with her heavy load of
game.

When Oowikapun reached the entrance to this part of the trail
he was surprised to notice the sudden disappearance of the tracks
of the catamount. Rapidly did his eyes scan every spot within
jumping distance, and still not a vestige of a footstep was visible.
But he was not to be deceived. Knowing the character of these
animals, he carefully examined the trunks of the trees close at
hand, and on one he found the marks of the creature's claws, as it
had sprung from the trail into it. This discovery added to the
excitement of Oowikapun, and caused him to be still more alert
and cautious. These animals can climb trees like squirrels, and
glide along from branch to branch with amazing celerity where
the trees are large. They seem to prefer to make their attack by
springing upon their victims from a tree rather than from the
ground, as their aim is to seize them by the throat. Oowikapun
was aware of this, and it added to his anxiety and alertness.

Once or twice he caught sight of the creature as, like a South American puma, it glided along from tree to tree. Soon he saw it pause for an instant, and become greatly agitated. It appeared to quiver with excitement. It was still a long shot from him, as he had only a smooth-bore, flintlock gun. The temptation to fire was great, but, wishing to be sure of his aim, he resolved to follow on and get so near that no second ball would be needed. On again glided the beast, and was soon lost to view, while Oowikapun followed as rapidly as he thought it was best in the crooked trail, when suddenly he heard the wild shriek that seemed to tell of the triumph of the savage beast. As he dashed on, a sharp turn in the trail showed him the bloodthirsty beast tearing at the back of a prostrate woman, upon whom he had sprung from the tree, and thrown to the ground.

With all an Indian's coolness and presence of mind Oowikapun knew that while he must act quickly, he must also guard against accidentally injuring the woman. So, raising his gun in position, he shouted out the Indian word for " Keep still ! " and as the beast raised his head at the unexpected sound, the bullet went crashing through his brain and he fell dead as a stone.

To rush forward to the woman he had rescued and ascertain the extent of her wounds was but the work of an instant. And that instant was all the woman required to spring up and see who it was that she had to thank for her sudden deliverance from such a terrible death.

Thus, face to face, they met again—Oowikapun and Astumastao. Reaching out her hand, while her bright eyes spoke more eloquently than words, she said,—

" I am very thankful for your coming, and for my speedy rescue ; and not less so when I see it has been by Oowikapun ! "

" Oowikapun is glad to be of any service to Astumastao," he said, as he took the proffered hand and held it ; while he added, " But are you not badly wounded ? "

" Only in my arm do I feel hurt," she replied.

On inspection it was found that the wounds there were made by the claws and not by the teeth, and so did not appear very serious.

As these very practical young people discussed the attack and escape, it was unanimously agreed that it was very fortunate for Astumastao that she had the heavy load of rabbits on her back, and several brace of partridges about her neck. When the brute sprang upon her he had only plunged his teeth and claws into the game.

We need not here go into the particulars of all the beautiful things which were said by these two very interesting young people. Human nature is about the same the world over. This is not a romantic love-story, even if it turns out to be a lovely story. Suffice it here to say that at first a fire was kindled, and the wounded arm was dressed and bandaged. Some balsam from the trees was easily obtained by Oowikapun for the purpose, and a warm wrapping of rabbit skins taken from the newly-caught animals sufficed to keep the cold from the wounds. These prompt and thorough Indian methods for curing wounds were most successful, and in a few days they were completely healed. When the dressing of the arm was attended to Oowikapun returned for his sled, which he had left at the spot where he first caught sight of the catamount, while Astumastao busied herself with cooking some of the game which she had caught, and which she had about ready when he returned.

Perhaps some of my more fastidious readers would not have cared much for a meal thus prepared and eaten without the use of plates or forks. But there are others who have dined in this way, and the remembrance of such meals, with the glorious appetite which forest or mountain air has given, is to them a delicious memory. This one, any way, was very much enjoyed by these sensible young people. When it was over, Oowikapun quickly skinned the catamount. He left the head attached to the skin, and placed it on his sled that it might be shown to the villagers when they arrived. The body he left behind as worthless, as it is never eaten by the Indians, although they are fond of the wild cats and some other carnivorous animals. Astumastao's load of game was also placed upon his sled, and then together they resumed their journey to the village.

Great was the excitement among the people when the story

became known, and in their Indian way they at once promoted Oowikapun to the ranks of the great " braves." He was by all considered quite a hero, and made welcome in all of the wigwams he chose to visit. The aunt of Astumastao welcomed him most cordially. Kissing him again and again, she called him her son, while she thanked him most gratefully for his noble deed. Gladly accepting her invitation, he repeated his visits to her wigwam as often as Indian etiquette would sanction.

One day, when only the three of them were present, Oowikapun, who had heard from some of the people of the heroic way in which Astumastao had rescued her uncle Kistayimoowin from a watery grave, asked her to tell him the story.

As a general thing, little reference is made among the Indians to the dead. Without any light to illumine the valley and shadow of death, the whole thing is so dreadful, that they never mention the word death. When obliged to speak of those who have gone, they say, " nou pimatissit," which means, " He is not among the living."

However, Astumastao and her aunt had none of these foolish notions, especially as since the sad event the aunt had eagerly drunk in all the information she could get from her niece, who now had none in the wigwam to crush her song or quiet her speech.

As Astumastao had a double object in view, she willingly described the scene as we have already done. She dwelt fully upon his calling for her to sing, and his longing to learn all he could about the name of Jesus. The recital produced a deep impression upon Oowikapun, and brought up all the memories of his own darkness and mental disquietude, while month after month he had been groping along in his vain attempts to find soul happiness.

During this interview she told him how she and her aunt had tried, ever since her uncle's death, to live in the way of the book of heaven, but that they knew so little, and there were so many mysteries and perplexities all around them, that they were at times much discouraged. But there was one thing they had resolved upon, and that was never to go back to the old pagan religion of their forefathers. They were happier in their minds now, with the glimmering light of the white man's way, than ever they had been in their lives before.

Oowikapun listened, and was encouraged. He told them fully of his own troubles, for he felt he had, for the first time, sympathetic listeners. When he described his various methods to get peace and quiet for his anxieties, and referred to the ceremony of torture through which he had gone, Astumastao's eyes flashed with indignation and then filled with tears. Strong words seemed about coming from her lips, but, with an effort, she controlled herself and remained quiet.

Very frequently did Oowikapun find his way to the wigwam where dwelt these two women, and doubtless many were the things about which they talked. For a time he visited the snares and traps and brought in the game. One day he returned with the splendid black fox, which Astumastao had tried so hard to capture. For this they gratefully thanked him, as well as for the great, tawny skin of the catamount, which he had carefully prepared as a splendid rug and spread out for them in their wigwam.

The wounded arm was now completely healed, and the business which Oowikapun had used as his excuse for coming to the village was long ago arranged. And still he lingered.

CHAPTER XII.

The same old story.—Oowikapun is in love with our heroine.—Indian courtship generally very short.—He seems to make but slow progress.—
Astumastao's reserve.—" All things come to him who waits."— He tells of
his affection for her.—His suit urged in vain.—She tells him of her brave
resolve to go for a missionary for her people.—Vainly Oowikapun pleads
for her to marry him, and for them both to go. Her refusal.— A dangerous undertaking.—Vainly Oowikapun expostulates.—His own brave,
sudden resolve.—He secretly leaves the village.

"HE ASKED HER TO MARRY HIM."

CHAPTER XII.

TO the villagers the cause was very evident, but why there should be any trouble or delay in his courtship they could not make out. Of course he would take Astumastao's aunt to live with them, and therefore there was no price to pay for the maiden. So quickly and promptly do the Indians attend to these things, that when matters have gone between their young folks, as they evidently imagined they had between these two, a decision one way or another is quickly reached.

These simple people do not believe in long courtships with a mitten at the end. So they began to wonder why this matter was not settled. They were nearly all very favourably inclined toward Oowikapun, and were pleased at the prospect of his marrying a maiden of their village. Even some of the young men who had hoped to have won her, when they heard the story of her wonderful deliverance by the fine young hunter of another village, and observed how he had set his heart upon her, retired from the field, saying that Oowikapun's claims to her were greater than theirs, and that for themselves they must look elsewhere. But while Astumastao's eyes brightened when Oowikapun entered the wigwam, and her welcome was always kindly, yet she skilfully changed the conversation when it seemed to be leading toward the tender sentiment. Women are more skilful than men, and she, for some reason, would never let him see that she appeared to think of him as a suitor. By her tact she kept him from saying what was in his heart.   And yet she was no mere coquette.   In her great loving heart was a purpose noble and firm, and a resolve so high, that for the present all other sentiments and feelings must hold a subordinate place.   So, while she did not repel him, or offend his sensitive spirit, she made him feel that he must defer a matter to him so important, and talk on other subjects.   There was one theme on which she was always eager to talk, and to her it never grew stale or threadbare.   It was about what he and she had learned of the book of heaven, and the good white man's way.

She sang her hymns to him, and called up happy memories of the year which she had spent in the home of the missionary. She made him tell her, over and over again, all he could remember of Memotas and Achimoowin, and, as well as she could in her quiet way, let him see how solicitous she was that he should try to find out how to get into this way.

Oowikapun was thankful for all this kindness, and was very happy in her presence.   But he was all the time getting more deeply in love with her, and, while anxious to learn all he could from her, had come to the sage conclusion that if she would marry him he could learn so much the faster.

It is said that "all things come to him who waits," and so the opportunity which our Indian friend had so long desired came to him at last.

Astumastao had been telling him one day when they were alone of the persecutions she had met with from her uncle, Koosapatum, and others, and then stated how hard it was for her alone to remember about the Good Book, and live up to its lessons.   Then she added, if there had only been some one among the people who knew more than she did to stand firm with her, they might have helped each other along, and been so firm and brave.

When she had finished, Oowikapun saw his opportunity, and was quick to avail himself of it.   He replied by deeply sympathising with her, and then, referring to his own difficulties and failures in the past, stated how fearful he was of the future unless he had some true, brave friend to help him along.   Then, suddenly facing her, in strong and loving words he urged her to be his teacher and helper, his counsellor—his wife.

So quickly had the conversation changed, and so suddenly had come this declaration, that Astumastao was thrown off her guard and more deeply agitated than perhaps she had ever been before.

However, she soon regained her composure, and replied to him not unkindly, but candidly and unmistakably. She said she was very sorry he had made such a request, for she had set her heart upon some work which would perhaps make it impossible for her to think of marriage for years to come.

Vainly he urged his suit. She was firm. He had the satisfaction of getting from her the information that at some future interview she would tell him of the great object she had set her heart upon, and he had to leave the wigwam feeling that his chances of winning Astumastao were not quite so bright as he vainly imagined.

As we may well suppose, Oowikapun was very anxious to know the reason which had so strong a hold upon Astumastao, and so, just as soon as Indian etiquette would allow another visit to her wigwam, he went there.

When some Indian maidens who had been learning from Astumastao some new designs in bead work, at which she was very skilful, had retired, and the two young people and the aunt were now left alone, in a straightforward manner she told what was uppermost in her heart. It was of a purpose which had been growing there for years, but which she had only seen the possibilities of carrying out since her uncle's death. She said she believed they ought to have a missionary to teach them the truths in the book of heaven. Pe-pe-qua-napuay, the new chief, was not unfriendly, as he had himself declared that he had lost faith in the old pagan way. And Koosapatum, the conjurer, had lost his power over the young men, who now feared not his threats; and at Tapastanum, the old medicine man, they even laughed when he threatened them. So she had resolved to go all the way to Norway House, to plead with the missionary there, to send away to the land of missionaries, and get one to come and live among them and be their teacher. She knew it

was far away, and her hands and arms would often get weary
with paddling her canoe, and her feet would get sore. Perhaps
the moccasins would wear out in the portages, where the stones
were sharp and the rocks many; but they had talked it all over
and they had resolved to go. Two women were to go with her.
One, who was a widow, was to be the guide. She had gone over
the way years ago with her husband, and thought that she could
remember the trail. The other was a young woman and a companion of Astumastao. From being much with her she longed
for more instruction. These two women, she said, were anxious
to go with her. They were sick of the way they were living,
and longed for the better life, and a knowledge of what was
beyond.

They had been making their preparations for a long time, she
said. A friendly family would keep the aunt in her absence,
and look after her little wigwam. They had been making bead
work, and some other things to sell at Norway House, so that
they would not be dependent upon the friends there while they
pleaded for a missionary.

Thus talked this noble girl. As she went on and described the
blessing that would come to her people if she should succeed,
she became so fired up with this noble resolve, which had taken
possession of her, that poor Oowikapun felt himself very guilty in
having dared to make a proposal of marriage, which would in
any way thwart a purpose so noble, and which might be followed
by such blessed results.

And yet when, alone and in cool blood, Oowikapun pondered
over the nature of the task she had decided to undertake, and
thought of the perils and difficulties in the way, he resolved
to try to persuade her to abandon the perilous undertaking.
Patiently she listened to all he had to say, but would not be
persuaded to abandon the scheme on which her heart was set.

Seeing this, he tried to arrange some compromise, or some
other plan. First he asked her to marry him and let him go
along in place of the young Indian maiden. This plan, which
seemed so agreeable to Oowikapun, she quickly dismissed, saying
that she did not intend to be married until she could be married

in the beautiful Christian way she remembered having seen when a child, and by a Christian missionary.

Failing in this scheme, Oowikapun suggested that he should select some strong young fellow, and that together they should set off as soon as the ice disappeared from the rivers, and present her request.

To this Astumastao replied, and there was a little tinge of banter, if not of sarcasm, as well as a good deal of seriousness, in her voice, " And suppose in one of the Indian villages through which you might pass, a sun or ghost dance, or even the ceremony of the devil worship or dog feast might be going on, who knows but you might be persuaded to jump into the magic circle and dance yourself senseless ? Or if you did not succeed, might you not in your discouragement go off again to the tortures and miseries of Hock-e-a-yum ?"

These words made him wince, but he could only feel that they were true, and that he deserved them all. He realised that until he did something to redeem himself in the eyes of this brave, true woman, he was only worthy of her reproofs.

Seeing that her words had so hurt him, the generous-hearted girl, who, while grieved at the failures he had made, could also appreciate his noble qualities and sympathise with him in his struggles for the light, quickly turned the conversation, and then, as though making a confidant of him, told him of all the plans of their contemplated journey.

One day while Oowikapun was pondering over the words of Astumastao, and thinking of the risks she and her companions were about to run, and the dangers they would have to encounter in their great undertaking, and contrasting it with the listless, aimless life he had lately been leading, there suddenly came to him a noble resolve. This took such possession of him and so enthused him that he appeared and acted like another man.

To carry it out was quickly decided upon, and so, letting no one know of his purpose, he very early, one crisp wintry morning, tied his little travelling outfit, with his axe and gun, upon his sled, and, without saying "good-bye" to any one, even to Astumastao, he secretly left the village.

CHAPTER XIII.

"THE YOUNG MEN AND MAIDENS OF THE VILLAGE TALKED," ETC

CHAPTER XIII.

THE mysterious disappearance of Oowikapun from the village of his friends caused a good deal of excitement and innocent gossip.

That he was deeply in love with Astumastao was evident to all, and while she did not allow even her most intimate friends to hear her say that she intended to marry him, yet her conduct very plainly indicated that he stood higher than any one else in her esteem. That she had positively rejected him, none of them could believe. Why, then, had he thus shown the white feather, and so ignominiously and so suddenly left the field when it seemed so evident that a little more perseverance would have surely resulted in his success. In this way the young men and maidens of the village talked, while the old men gravely smoked their calumets, and mourned that the times were so changed that a young brave should have so much trouble in capturing a squaw.

When Astumastao was informed of the sudden disappearance of Oowikapun she was troubled and perplexed. Not the slightest hint had he given her of his intended movements, when, like a flash, there had come to him the great resolve to be the one who should go on the long journey to find the missionary. She was a maiden not beautiful, but she was a comely Indian girl, attractive and clever in her way, and she well knew that many a young hunter had sat down beside her wigwam door, or had dropped the shining white pebble before her in the path, thus plainly intimating their desire to win her notice and esteem. But to all of them she had turned a deaf ear, and had treated them, without exception, with perfect indifference. As shy and timid as a young fawn of the forest, she had lived under the watchful and somewhat jealous care of her uncle and aunt, until Oowikapun had appeared in the village.

His coming, however, and his reference to Memotas, had strangely broken the quiet monotony of years. Then what she had done for him in the wigwam, their conversation in the trail, and, above all, his gallant rescue of her from the terrible catamount, had aroused new emotions within her and opened up her mind to a wider vision, until now she saw that she was no longer the young free Indian girl, with no thoughts but those of her childhood, but a woman who must now act and decide for herself. But, with the characteristic reserve of her people, she kept all these new-born emotions and aspirations hid in her heart.

The power to control the feelings and passions among the Indians is not confined to the sterner sex. Schooled in a life of hardship, the women as well as the men can put on the mask of apparent indifference, while at the same time the heart is racked by intensest feeling, or the body is suffering most horrid torture. Death in its most dreadful form may be staring them in the face, and yet an outsider may look in vain for the blanching of the cheek, or the quivering of a muscle. Very early in life does this stern education begin.

" That is my best child," said an Indian father, as he pointed out an apparently happy little girl of seven or eight years old, in his wigwam.

" Why should she be your favourite child ? " was asked him.

" Why ? because she, of all my children, will go the longest without food without crying," was his answer.

To suffer, but to show no sign, is the proverb of the true Indian. And yet Astumastao would not admit even to herself that she was so deeply in love with Oowikapun.

She had treasured the fond conceit in her heart, that the one all-absorbing passion with her was that which she had freely revealed to him, and she in her simplicity had honestly believed that no other love could take its place, or even share the room in her heart.

But here was a rude awakening. She was a mystery to herself. Why these sighs, and tears, when alone and unwatched by her bright-eyed, alert, young associates? Why did the image of this one young Indian hunter intrude itself so persistently before her in her waking hours? It is true he came not frequently to her in her dreams, for we dream but little of those we love the most, and who are in our memories and on our hearts continually during the waking hours of active life.

Untaught in the schools, and free from all the guiles of heartless coquetry, an orphan girl in an Indian village, with neither prudence on the one hand nor premature hot-house teaching on the other, which turns the heads of so many girls, Astumastao was to herself a riddle which she could not solve— a problem the most difficult of any she had ever tried to understand.

Her maidenly modesty seemed first to tell her to banish his image from her heart, and his name from her lips. To accomplish this she threw herself with renewed diligence into the duties incident to her simple yet laborious life, and by her very activities endeavoured to bring herself back to the sweet simplicities of her earlier days. But fruitless were all her efforts. The heart transfixed was too strong for the head, and the new love, which had so unconsciously come to her, would not be stilled or banished.

A true daughter of Eve was this forest maiden, even if she did live in a wigwam, and had never read a novel or a romance; and because she had these feelings, and was passing through these hours of disquietude and conflicting emotions, we think none the less of her. Our only regret is that she had no wise, judicious friend of her own sex, to whom in her perplexity she could have gone for wise and prudent council. Happy are those daughters in civilised lands who have their precious mothers, or other safe counsellors, to whom they can go in these crucial hours of their

history, when their future weal or woe may turn upon the
decisions then made. And happy are those fair maidens who,
instead of impulsively and recklessly rejecting all counsel and
warning from their truest friends, listen to the voice of experience
and parental love, and, above all, seek aid from the infinitely
loving One who has said : "If any of you lack wisdom, let him
ask of God that giveth to all men liberally and withholdeth not ;
and it shall be given him."

Astumastao, unfortunately, had no one to whom she could go
in her perplexity. Her feeble aunt had been a purchased wife,
bought in the long ago by her husband, whom she had never
seen until the day when he had come from a distant village, and,
being impressed with her appearance—for she was then a fine-
looking young woman—had quickly spread out at her father's
feet all the gifts he demanded for her. His first words to her
were to inform her that she was his wife, and that very shortly
they would set out for his distant home. Crushed out of her
heart were some feelings of affection for a handsome young hunter,
who had several times met her on the trail, as she was accustomed to go to the bubbling spring, in the shady dell, for water
for her father's wigwam. Few, indeed, had been his words, but
his looks had been bright and full of meaning, and he had let her
know that he was gathering up the gifts that would purchase
her from her stern and avaricious father. But alas ! her dreams
and hopes had been blasted, and her heart crushed by this old
pagan custom ; and so for long years she had lived the dreary,
monotonous life to which we have referred. Such a woman could
give no advice that would be of much service to such an alert,
thoughtful girl as Astumastao ; and so, unaided and undisciplined,
she let her thoughts drift, and her heart became the seat of
emotions and feelings most diverse. Sometimes she bitterly
upbraided herself for her coldness and indifference to Oowikapun,
as she thought of his many noble qualities. Then, again, she
would marshal before her his weaknesses and defects, and would
vainly try to persuade herself to believe that the man who had
been in the tent of Memotas and had heard him pray, and had
then gone into the devil dance and had voluntarily suffered the

tortures of Hock-e-a-yum, was unworthy of her notice. Then suddenly, as the memory of what he must have suffered in those terrible ordeals came before her, her bright eyes would fill up with tears, and she found herself impulsively longing for the opportunity to drive the recollection of such sufferings from his mind and heart, and to be the one to save him from their repetition.

Amidst these conflicting emotions there was one thought that kept coming up in her mind and giving her much trouble, and that was—" Why had he left so abruptly? Why did he not at least come and say 'Good-bye'? or why had he not left at least some little message for her?"

Over these queries she pondered, and they were more than once thrown at her by the young Indian maidens, as with them she was skilfully decorating with beads some snow-white moccasins she had made.

Thus pondered Astumastao through the long weeks that were passing by since Oowikapun left her; while he, brave fellow, little dreaming that such conflicting feelings were in her heart, was putting his life in jeopardy, and enduring hardships innumerable, to save and benefit the one who had become dearer to him than life itself.

Thus the time rolled on, and all of her efforts to banish him from her mind proved failures, and it came to pass that, like the true, noble girl that she was, she could only think of that which was brave and good about him; and so, when some startling rumours of a delightful character began to be circulated among the wigwams, our heroine Astumastao, without knowing the reason why, at once associated them with Oowikapun.

News travels rapidly sometimes, even in lands where telegraphs and express trains are unknown. It does not always require the well-appointed mail service to carry the news rapidly through the land.

During the terrible civil war in the United States there was, among the negroes of the South, what was known as the grape vine telegraphy, by which the coloured people in remote sections often had news of success or disaster to the army of " Uncle

Abraham," as they loved to call President Lincoln, long before the whites had any knowledge of what had occurred.

So it is among the Indian tribes. In some mysterious, and, to the whites, most unaccountable way, the news of success or disaster was carried hundreds of miles in a marvellously short period of time. For example, the defeat and death of General Custer, at the battle of the Rosebud, was known among the Sioux Indians near St. Paul's for several hours before the military authorities at the same place had any knowledge of it, although the whites were able to communicate more than half of the way with each other by telegraph. An interesting subject this might prove for some one, who had time, and patience, to give it a thorough investigation.

The rumours of coming blessings to the people kept increasing. At length they assumed a form so tangible that the people began to understand what was meant. It seems that some hunters met some other hunters in their far-off wanderings, who had come across a party of Norway House Christian Indians, who informed them that a visit might be soon expected from the white man, with the great Book, about which there had been so many strange things circulating for such a long time. When Astumastao heard these rumours, she was excited and perplexed. While hoping most sincerely that they were true, and would speedily be fulfilled, yet she could not but feel that she would have rejoiced if she had been able to have made the long journey for which she had been so industriously preparing, and had had something to do in bringing the missionary and the Book among her own people. And then she let her thoughts go to some one else, and she said to herself: "I will so rejoice if it turns out to be the work of dear Oowikapun."

CHAPTER XIV.

Missionary work among the Northern Indians.—Norway House one of the
earliest and most successful.—Other tribes longing for the same blessings.—Many deputations from other places.—Pleadings of the old
man.—" My eyes have grown dim through long watching."—Immense
mission-fields.—Hardships and privations of the workers.—Two welcome
visitors at the mission house.—Memotas and Oowikapun.—Our hero in
the presence of the missionary.—How had he reached that place?—The
story of his trip.—Many adventures.—One supper on marrow-bones left
by the wolves.—Rescued an old man deserted by his friends and left to
be devoured by the wolves.—Welcomed in the home of Memotas.

"'MY SAFEST PLAN WAS TO GET UP INTO A TREE.'"

CHAPTER XIV.

THE success which has attended the efforts of the missionaries in preaching the gospel among the most northern tribes of Indians has been very encouraging. For a long time they had been dissatisfied with their old paganism. They had in a measure become convinced that their religious teachers, their medicine men, and conjurers were impostors, and so, while submitting somewhat to their sway through fear, were yet chafing under them. When the first missionaries arrived among them, they were soon convinced that they were their true friends. Not only were they men of purest character, but they were men who practically sympathised with the people. To the full measure of their ability, and often beyond, they helped the sick and suffering ones, and more than once divided their last meal with the poor, hungry creatures, who came to them in their hours of direst need.

The result was, that the people were so convinced of the genuineness of these messengers of peace and goodwill, that large numbers of them gladly accepted the truth and became Christians. The story of the founding of these missions went far and wide throughout all these northern regions, and at many a distant camp-fire, and in many a wigwam hundreds of miles away, the red men talked of the white man, and his book of heaven.

Occasionally some of these hunters or trappers from the still remote pagan districts, would meet with some of the Christian hunters from the missions, and from them would learn something of the great salvation revealed in the book of heaven, and would return more dissatisfied than ever with their old sinful pagan ways.

Then it sometimes happened that a missionary, full of zeal for his Master and of sympathy for these neglected souls in the wilderness, would undertake long journeys into their country to preach the gospel. Many were the hardships and dangers of those trips, which were often of many weeks' duration. They were made in summer in a birch canoe, in company with a couple of noble Christian Indians. They were not only able to skilfully paddle the canoe and guide it safely down the swift, dangerous rapids and carry it across the portages, but were also of great help to the missionary in spreading the gospel, by telling of their own conversion, and of the joy and happiness which had come to them through the hearty acceptance of this way.

In winter, the missionary could only make these long journeys by travelling with dogs, accompanied by a faithful guide, and some clever dog-drivers. Sometimes they travelled for three hundred miles through the cold forests, or over the great frozen lakes, for many days together, without seeing a house. When night overtook them, they dug a hole in the snow, and there they slept or shivered as best they could. Their food was fat meat, and they fed their dogs on fish. The cold was so terrible that, sometimes, every part of their faces exposed to the dreadful cold was frozen. Once the nose and ears of one of the missionaries froze in bed. Often the temperature ranged from forty to sixty degrees below zero. It was perhaps the hardest mission-field in the world as regards the physical sufferings and privations endured. But, fired by a noble ambition to preach the gospel " in the regions beyond," these men of God considered no suffering too severe, or difficulties insurmountable, if only they could succeed.

They were among those of whom it is said :

> " Fired with a zeal peculiar, they defy
> The rage and rigour of a northern sky,
> And plant successfully sweet Sharon's rose
> On icy fields amidst eternal snows."

Wherever they could gather the wandering Indians together, even in little companies, for religious service, they did so. On the banks of the lakes or rivers, in the forests, at their camp-fires, or in their wigwams, they ceased not to speak, and to preach Jesus. The result was a spirit of enquiry was abroad, and so in spite of the old conjurers and medicine men, who were determined, if possible, not to lose their grip upon them, there was a longing to know more and more about this better way.

Norway House Mission was the spot to which many eyes were directed, and to which deputations asking for missionary help often came. It was the largest and most flourishing of those northern missions, and for years had its own printing-press and flourishing schools. Very pathetic and thrilling were some of the scenes in connexion with some of these importunate Indian deputations, who came from remote regions to plead with the resident missionary that they might have one of their own, to live among them and help them along in the right way.

One deputation consisting of old men came year after year, and when still refused each successive year, because there were none to volunteer for a life so full of hardships, and no money in the missionary treasury, even if a man could be found, became filled with despair, and even bitterness, and said : "Surely, then, the white men do not, as they say, consider us as their brothers, or they would not leave us without the book of heaven, and one of their number to show us the true way."

Another old man, with bitterness of soul and tremulousness of speech, when replying to the refusal of his request for a missionary for his people, said : "My eyes have grown dim with long watching, and my hair has grown grey while longing for a missionary."

These important appeals, transmitted year after year to the missionary authorities, at length aroused the churches. More help was sent, but not before the toilers on the ground had almost killed themselves in their work. Vast, indeed, was the area of some of those mission fields, and wretched and toilsome were the methods of travel over them. George McDougall's mission was larger than all France, Henry Steinhaur's was larger than Germany, the one of which Norway House was the principal station was over five hundred miles long and three hundred wide, and there were others just as large. No wonder men quickly broke down and had to retire from such work. The prisoners in the jails and penitentiaries of the land live on much better fare than did these heroic men and their families. The great staple of the north was fish. Fish twenty-one times a week for six months, and not much else with it. True, it was sometimes varied by a pot of boiled musk-rat, or a roasted leg of a wild-cat.

Yet amidst such hardships, which tried both souls and bodies, they toiled on bravely and uncomplainingly, and as far as possible responded to the pleading Macedonian calls that came to them for help from the distant regions still farther beyond, and gladly welcomed to their numbers the additional helpers when they arrived.

With only one of these deputations pleading for a missionary have we here to do.

It was a cold, wintry morning. The fierce storms of that northern land were howling outside, and the frost-king seemed to be holding high carnival. Quickly and quietly was the door of the mission house opened and in there came two Indians. One of them was our beloved friend Memotas, who was warmly greeted by all, for he was a general favourite. The little children of the mission home, Sagastaookemou and Minnehaha, rushed into his arms, and kissed his bronzed but handsome face. When their noisy greetings were over, he introduced the stranger who was with him. He seemed to be about twenty-seven or twenty-eight years of age, and was a handsome-looking man; in fact, an ideal Indian of the forest. Very cordially was he welcomed, and Memotas said his name was Oowikapun.

Thus was our hero in the mission house, and in the presence of the first missionary he had ever seen. How had he reached this place, and what was his object in coming? These questions, which excite our curiosity, we will try to answer.

The last glimpse we had of Oowikapun was when he was quietly speeding away from the far-off village, where dwelt Astumastao, and, according to the hunters who were returning, not in the trail leading to his own village. His presence here in the mission house, hundreds of miles in the opposite direction, now explains to us the way in which he must have travelled.

From his own lips, long after, the story of his adventurous trip was told.

Oowikapun said that when he left Astumastao after that last interview, in which he so completely failed to divert her from her determination to undertake, with the other women, the long, dangerous journey, and in which she had shown him how little he was to be depended upon, he went back to the wigwam of his friends feeling very uncomfortable. His relatives had all gone off hunting or visiting, and so, there he was, alone in his tent. He kindled a fire, and there by it he sat, and tried to think over what had happened, and was full of regret at what Astumastao had resolved to do. While almost frightened at the dangers she was about to face, he could not but be proud of her spirit and courage.

Then the thought came to him, "What are you doing? Is there not man enough in you, to do this work, and save these women from such risks? Is it not as much for you as anybody else the missionary is needed? Are you not about the most miserable one in the tribe? Here is your opportunity to show what you can accomplish. As Memotas was always doing the hard work for his wife, here is your chance to save from danger and serve that one you are longing to call your wife."

"While I thought about it," said Oowikapun, "the thing took took such hold upon me, that it fairly made me tremble with excitement, and I resolved to set about it at once. So I quickly gathered my few things together, and when all was still I left the village. Some falling snow covered up my snowshoe tracks, and the little trail made by my sled, and so no one could tell in which direction I had gone."

Continuing, Oowikapun said : " I had many adventures. The snow was very deep, but I had my good snowshoes and plenty of ammunition, and as there was considerable game, I managed very well. One night I had a supper of marrow bones, which I got hold of in a strange way. I was pushing along early in the forenoon, when I heard a great noise of wolves, not very far off.

9

Quickly I unstrapped my gun and prepared to defend myself, if
I should be attacked. Their howlings so increased, I became
convinced that they were so numerous that my safest plan was to
get up in a tree as quickly as possible. This I did, and then drew
my sled beyond their reach. Not very long after I had succeeded
in this, I saw a great moose deer plunging through the deep snow,
followed by fierce grey wolves. He made the most desperate efforts
to escape, but, as they did not sink deeply in the snow while
he broke through at every plunge, they were too much for him.
Although he badly injured some of them, yet they succeeded in
pulling him down and devoured him. It was dreadful to see the
way they snarled and fought with each other over the great body.
They gorged themselves ere they went away, and left nothing but
the great bones. When they had disappeared, I came down from
the tree, in which I had been obliged to remain about six hours. I
was nearly frozen, and so I quickly cut down some small dead
trees, and make up a good fire. I then gathered the large
marrow bones, from which the wolves had gnawed the meat, and
standing them up against a log close to the fire, I roasted them
until the marrow inside was well cooked. Then cracking them
open with the back of my axe, I had a famous supper upon what
the wolves had left.

"I had several other adventures," said Oowikapun, "but the
most interesting of all, and the one most pleasing to me, was that
I reached Beaver Lake in time to rescue an old man from being
eaten by the wolves. His relatives were some very heartless
people of the Saulteaux tribe. They were making a long journey
through the country to a distant hunting ground, and because this
old grandfather could not keep up in the trail, and food was not
very plentiful, they deliberately left him to perish. They acted
in a very cruel and heartless way. They stuck some poles in the
snow, and then over the top they threw a few pieces of birch bark.
This, in mockery, they called his tent. Then seating him on a
log in it, where he was exposed to view on every side, they left him
without fire or blankets, and gave him only a small quantity of
dried meat in a birch dish, which they call a roggan. There, when
he had eaten his meat, he was expected to lie down and die.

"When I found him," said Oowikapun, "he was nearly dead with the cold. He had eaten his meat, and was sitting there on the log, brandishing his old tomahawk to keep off several wolves who were sitting around him just outside of the circle of his weapon, patiently waiting until he would become wearied out, when they would spring in upon him and speedily devour him." So intent were they on watching him, that Oowikapun said he was able to get up so close to them that he sent the bullet through two of them, killing them instantly. The others, frightened by the report of the gun, quickly rushed away. "I cheered up the old man," said Oowikapun, "and speedily made a fire and gave him some warm soup, which I prepared. I had to stay there with him a day before he was strong enough to go on with me to Norway House by dragging him on my sled most of the way. I took him to the house of Memotas, where he was kindly treated and cared for, as are all who come under the roof of that good man."

CHAPTER XV.

"HE SENT THE BULLET THROUGH TWO OF THEM.

CHAPTER XV.

DURING the days and weeks following, Oowikapun pleaded for a missionary, and had a great helper in Memotas, who had become much interested in him. This devoted man had often thought about the young wounded Indian who long ago had come to his hunting lodge to be cured of the injuries inflicted by the savage wolf.

Since his arrival, he had drawn from him many of the events that had occurred in his life since they two had kneeled down in the woods together. He had opened to Memotas his heart, and had told him of his feeble efforts to live the better life, and of his complete failure.

He told him of Astumastao, and made the heart of Memotas and others glad, who remembered the little black-eyed girl from the far north, who had dwelt a year in the village. They all rejoiced to hear that she still treasured in her breast so much of the truth, and was so anxious for a missionary. These were happy weeks for Oowikapun. Under the faithful instructions of Memotas he was being rapidly helped along in the way to a Christian life. Perplexities and mysteries were being cleared away, and light was driving the darkness and gloom out of his mind. Frequently did the faithful missionary, who had also become much interested in him, have long conversations with him, and gave him much assistance, as well as arranging for the comfort of the old Salteaux whom he had rescued from such a dreadful death.

The plan of salvation by faith in the Lord Jesus was unfolded to Oowikapun, and the necessity of a firm and constant reliance upon God for help in times of need was so explained to him that he saw where his failures had been. In his own strength he had tried to resist temptation, and thus had sadly failed.

The Sabbath services intensely interested him, and soon in them he took great delight. The Sunday-school was to him a revelation, and he gladly accepted the invitation of Memotas, and became an interested member of his class. He seemed to live in a new world. When he contrasted what he had witnessed nearly all of his days amidst the darkness and evils of the pagan Indians with what he saw among these happy Christian people, his dream came up vividly before him, and had a new meaning.

Here, in this Christian village, were the people of his own race in the bright and happy way, with Jesus as their guide, and the beautiful heaven beyond as their destination.

As he studied them, the more importunate and anxious he became to have the missionary of this mission go and visit his people, and thus prepare the way for their own missionary, when he should come to live among them.

Oowikapun's anxiety for light, and his intense interest in everything that pertained to the progress of the people, and, above all, his resolve to succeed in getting the missionary, created a great deal of interest among the villagers. With their usual open-hearted hospitality, they invited him to their comfortable little homes, and from many of them he learned much to help him along in the good way.

So marvellously had Christianity lifted up and benefited the people that Oowikapun, with his simple forest ways, at times felt keenly his ignorance, as he contrasted his crude life with what he now witnessed. A genuine civilisation had come to many of these once degraded tribes, and now comfortable homes, and large and happy family circles, are to be found where not a generation ago all was dark and degraded, and the sweet word, home, was utterly unknown.

The conversion of some of these Indians was very remarkable, and the recital of how they had come out of the darkness into light was helpful to him. When there is a disposition to surrender, we are easily conquered. Such was the condition of mind of the missionary, to whom Oowikapun had come with his earnest appeals.

He resolved to go. This decision was no sooner reached than preparations began for a journey which would occupy at least a month. Four dog-trains had to be taken. A train consists of four dogs harnessed up in tandem style. The sleds are about ten feet long and sixteen inches wide. They are made of two oak boards, and are similar in construction to, but much stronger than, the sleds used on toboggan slides.

There are various breeds of dogs used in that country, but the most common are the Esquimaux. They are strong and hardy, and, when well trained, are capital fellows for their work ; but they are incorrigible thieves, and unmitigated nuisances. Other breeds have been introduced into the country, such as the St. Bernard and the Newfoundland. They all have the good qualities of the Esquimaux, and are happily free from their blemishes. Some few Scottish stag-hounds, and other dogs of the hound varieties, have been brought in by Hudson Bay officers; but, while they make very swift trains and can be used for short trips, they are too tender to stand the bitter cold, and the long and difficult journeys through those desolate regions.

The various articles for the long journey were speedily gathered together, and the sleds carefully packed. Preparing for such a journey is a very different thing from getting ready for a trip in a civilised land. Here the missionary and his Indian companions were going about three hundred miles into the wilderness, where they would not see a house or any kind of a human habitation from the day they left their homes until they reached their destination. They would not see the least vestige of a road. They would make their own trail on snowshoes all that distance, except when on the frozen lakes and rivers, when snowshoes would be exchanged for skates by some, while the others used their moccasins. Every night, when the toilsome day's travel was over, they would have to sleep in the snow in their own bed, which they carried with them. Their meals they must cook at camp-fires, which they would build when required, as they hurried along. So we can easily see that a variety of things would have to be packed on the four dog-sleds. Let us watch the experienced guide, and the dog-drivers, as they attend to this work.

The heaviest item of the load is the supply of fish for the dogs. As this trip is to be such a long one, each sled must carry over two hundredweight of fish alone. Then the food for the missionary and his Indians, which consists principally of fat meat, is the next heaviest item. Then there are the kettles and axes and dishes, and numerous robes and blankets and changes of clothing, and a number of other things to be ready for every emergency or accident. They are going to live so isolated from the rest of the world, that they must be entirely independent of it. One thing more they must not forget, and that is a liberal supply of dog-shoes; and so on this trip they take over a hundred.

In selecting his Indian companions, the missionary's first thought is for a suitable guide, as much depends on him. The one chosen for this trip was called Murdo, a very reliable man, who had come originally from Nelson river. Very clever and gifted are some of these northern guides. Without the vestige of a track before them, and without the mark of an axe upon a tree, or the least sign that human beings had ever passed that way before, they stride along on their big snowshoes, day after day, without any hesitancy. The white man often gets so bewildered, that he does not know east from west, or north from south; but the guide never hesitates, and is very seldom at fault. To them it makes no difference whether the sun shines or clouds obscure the sky, or whether they journey by day or night. Sometimes it is necessary to do much of the travelling by night, on account of the reflection of the dazzling rays of the sun on the brilliant wastes of snow giving travellers snow-blindness, which is painful in the extreme. The sleep secured when thus travelling is during the hours of sunshine.

Yet the experienced guide will lead on just as well by night as by day. To him it makes no difference what may be the character of the night. Stars may shine, auroras may flash and scintillate, the moon may throw her cold, silvery beams over the landscape, or clouds may gather, and wintry storms rage and howl through the forest, yet on and on will the guide go, with unerring accuracy, leading to the desired camping-ground. With this guide, three dog-drivers, Oowikapun, and sixteen dogs, the missionary commenced his first journey to Nelson river.

The contemplated trip had caused no little excitement. This was not only on account of its dangers, but also because it was the pioneering trip for new evangelistic work among a people who had never seen a missionary or heard the name of Jesus. And so it was that although the start was made very early in the morning, yet there were scores of Indians gathered to see the missionary and his party off, and to wish them "God-speed" in their glorious work. The hasty "farewells" were soon said, and, parting from his loved ones, whom he would not see for a month, the missionary gave the word to start, and they were off.

Murdo, the guide, ran on ahead on his snowshoes. The missionary came next. He had with him Oowikapun, the happiest man in the crowd. When the missionary could ride, which was the case where the route lay over frozen lakes or along stretches of the rivers, Oowikapun was his driver, and rejoiced at being thus honoured. Following the missionary's train came the other three in single file, so that those following had the advantage of the road made by the sleds and snowshoes in front. Where the snow was very deep, or a fresh supply had recently fallen, it sometimes happened that the men had to strap on their snowshoes, and, following in the tracks of the guide, tramp on ahead of the dogs, and thus make a road over which those faithful animals could drag their heavy loads.

When our travellers began to feel hungry a fire was kindled, a kettle of tea prepared, and a hearty lunch of cold meat or pemmican was eaten and washed down with the strong tea. So vigorous are the appetites in that cold land that often five times a day do the travellers stop for lunch. Then on they go until the setting sun tells them it is time to prepare for the wintry camp where the night is to be spent. If possible to find, they select a place where there are green balsam trees, and plenty of dry, dead ones. The green ones will furnish the bed, while the dry ones will make the fire. When such a place is found, a halt is called, and everybody is busy. The dogs are quickly unharnessed, and gambol about close to the camp, and never attempt to desert.

From the spot selected for the camp, the snow is quickly scraped by using the great snowshoes as shovels. Then a roaring fire is made, and on it the kettles, filled with snow, are placed. In the larger kettle a piece of fat meat is cooked, and in the other one tea is made. While supper is cooking, the dogs are given their only daily meal. Two good whitefish constitute a meal. These are thawed out for them at the fire. After eating they curl themselves up in their nests, and sleep or shiver through the cold night as best they can. The supper, which consists principally of fat meat, is then eaten, and, after prayer, preparations are made for retiring. A layer of balsam boughs is placed on the ground; on this the robes and blankets are spread, and then the missionary, wrapping himself up in all the garments he can well get on, retires first, and is well covered up by additional blankets and fur robes. So completely tucked in is he that it is a mystery why he does not smother to death. But somehow he manages to survive, and after awhile gets so that he can stand it like an Indian. Persons unacquainted with this kind of life can hardly realise how it is possible for human beings to lie down in a hole in the snow, and sleep comfortably with the temperature everywhere from forty to sixty below zero. However, difficult as it is, it has to be done, if the gospel is to be carried to people, so remote, that there is no better way of reaching them. Such travellers are always thankful when a foot or eighteen inches of snow falls on them. It is a capital comforter, and adds very much to their warmth.

One of the most difficult things in connection with this kind of travelling is the getting up. The fire which was burning brightly when they retired was but a flashy one, and expired very soon, and did not long add to their comfort. And now when morning has come, and they have to spring up from their warm robes and blankets, the cold is so terrible that they suffer very much. No wonder they shiver and quickly get to work. Soon a roaring fire is burning, and breakfast prepared and enjoyed. After morning prayers, the sleds are packed, the dogs are harnessed, and the journey is resumed.

Eight times was the wintry camp made on this long trip, which was full of strange adventures, and many hardships; to every one of the party. Glad, indeed, were they, when Murdo and Oowikapun told the others, on the ninth day, at about noon, that they were only six miles from Nelson river.

CHAPTER XVI.

The trip ended.—A cordial welcome by the great majority of the people.—
In from their hunting-grounds.—The missionary visits the tent of the
savage old conjurer Koosapatum.—A surly welcome.—Won at last.—
Astumastao's joy at the arrival of a missionary.—The meeting of our
hero and heroine.—The picturesque assembly.—The first sermon.--The
rapt attention.—The hearty reception of the truth.—The response of the
chief and the people.

"THE OLD FELLOW WAS CROSS AND SURLY."

CHAPTER XVI.

THIS was welcome news to all. It was especially so to the missionary. He had not had the severe physical training which naturally falls to the lot of an Indian. True, he had his own dog sled, and was supposed to ride when possible, but there were whole days when he had to strap on his snowshoes and march along in single file with his Indians. As Oowikapun put it in his broken English, "Good missionary help make um track."

The result of this "make um track" business, was that he was about worn out, ere the journey was ended. Several times had the cramps seized him in such a way that the muscles of his legs gathered up in knots, and he suffered intensely for hours. Then his feet were so tender, that they chafed under the deerskin thongs of the snowshoes, and the blood soaked through his moccasins, and in many places crimsoned the snow, as he bravely toiled along. More than once, as he had to stop and rest on. a log covered with snow, did he question with himself whether he had done right in undertaking a journey so fraught with sufferings and dangers.

Cheering, then, was the news that the journey was so nearly ended. A halt was called, a good kettle of tea was prepared, and lunch was eaten with great pleasure. The dog-drivers put on some extra articles of finery of beautiful beadwork, that they might appear as attractive as possible.

Very cordially was the missionary and his party welcomed by the great majority of the people. They were very much interested and excited when they found that the first missionary with the book of heaven was among them. As many of the people were away hunting, runners were dispatched for those within reach. All of these northern Indians live by hunting. They are beyond the agricultural regions. Their summers are very short. The result is they know but little of farinaceous or vegetable food. There are old people there who never saw a potato or a loaf of bread. Their food is either the fish from the waters, or the game from the forests. The result is they have to wander around almost continually in search of these things. The missionaries have learned this, and endeavour to arrange their visits so as to meet them at their gatherings, in places where they assemble on account of the proximity of game. While these meeting places are called villages, they do not bear much resemblance to those of civilisation.

As soon as the missionary had rested a little, he paid a visit to the tent of Koosapatum, because he had quickly heard of the dire threats of the old sinner. So gloomy was the interior of the wigwam that, as the visitor pulled back the dirty deerskin which served as a door and entered, he could hardly see whether there was anybody in or not. No kindly word of greeting did he hear. However, his eyes soon got accustomed to the place, and then he was able to observe that the old conjurer and his wife were seated on the ground, on the opposite side of the tent. With some tea and tobacco in his left hand the missionary extended his right, saying, " What cheer, mismis?" the Indian for " How are you, grandfather?"

The old fellow was cross and surly, and most decidedly refused to shake hands, while he growled out some words of annoyance, and even threatening, at the coming of a missionary among his people.

The missionary, however, was not to be so easily rebuffed. Reaching down he took hold of his hand and, in a pump-handle sort of style, gave it quite a shaking. Then taking up the tobacco which with the tea he had dropped upon the ground, he quickly

placed it in the hand of the morose old man.   At first he refused
to take it.   But the missionary spoke kindly to him, and after a
little, as he had been out of the stuff for days, his fingers closed on
it ; and then the missionary knew that he had conquered in the
first skirmish.   Tobacco among these Indians is like salt among
the Arabs.   Knowing this the missionary, who never used
it himself, adopted this plan to make friends with the old
conjurer.

After he had taken the tobacco, the visitor took up the package
of tea and, looking at the dirty strips of meat which hung drying
over a stick, said : " You have meat, and I have tea.   If you will
furnish the meat, I will the tea, and we will have supper
together."

The first thought of the old sinner, as he glanced at his
medicine bag in which he kept his poisons, was, " What a good
chance I will now have to poison this man who has come to check
my power."   But the missionary saw that wicked gleam, and,
being well able to read these men by this time, quickly said,
" Never mind your medicine bag and your poisons.   I am your
friend, even if you do not believe it.   I have come into your
wigwam, and you have taken my tobacco, and I offer to eat and
drink with you ; and poison me *you dare not !* "

Thoroughly cowed and frightened that the white man had so
completely read his thoughts, he turned to his wife, and, in im-
perative tones, ordered her to quickly prepare the meat and the
tea.   So expeditiously was the work accomplished that it was not
very long ere the conjurer and missionary were eating and drink-
ing together.   The old fellow said the meat was venison ; the
missionary thought it was dog meat, and still thinks so.

Perhaps we cannot do better here than to anticipate the work a
little, and say that, at some later visits, this old conjurer was
induced to give up all of his wicked practices and become an
earnest Christian.

He so highly prized the visits of the missionary that he followed
him like his shadow.   He attended all the services.   When
wearied out with the day's toil and he prepared to rest, Koosapatum was not far off; and when the missionary kneeled down to

say his evening prayer alone, the now devout old man would kneel beside him and say, " Missionary, please pray out loud, and pray in my language, so that I can understand you."

Thus the gospel had come to the heart, and was influencing the life, of the conjurer of the Nelson River Indians. The service at which a great majority of the people decided for Christ was a very memorable one. It began at about eight o'clock in the morning. The majority of the Indians in all that vast district were gathered there.

Oowikapun's people were among the crowd, much to his delight. Astumastao and her aunt had heard of the gathering, and required no second invitation to be on hand. Great, indeed, was her joy to again look into the face, and hear the voice, of a missionary. Very much surprised and bewildered was she at having been anticipated by some one who had succeeded in bringing in the missionary, before she had begun her journey for this purpose. And great, indeed, was her joy and delight, and deeply was she moved, when she heard of the part Oowikapun had played in the important work.

The meeting between the two was genuine and natural. The dream of her youth was now accomplished, for here, ready to begin the religious service, was the missionary with the Good Book. His coming was the result of the efforts of Oowikapun. That she really loved him, the conflicts of the last few weeks most satisfactorily answered. His bronzed, weather-beaten appearance showed something of the hardships of the long journey, while his bright, happy face revealed to all, how amply repaid he felt for all he had endured and suffered.

As he entered the gathering assembly, and greeted friends and acquaintances, it was evident to all that his quick eager eyes were on the lookout for some special friend.

Not long had he to look. Astumastao, and her aunt, had come in from another wigwam, and were not very far behind him, and so were able to see how eagerly he was scanning the faces of those who had already assembled. So absorbed was he that the noiseless moccasined feet of others coming in behind him, were unnoticed.

For a moment she watched his wistful looks, and then, advancing towards him, with flushed but radiant face, she cordially exclaimed,—

" My brave Oowikapun ! "

Startled, overjoyed, and unconscious or careless of the hundreds of bright eyes that were on him, he seized the extended hand, and drawing her towards him, he imprinted upon her brow a kiss of genuine and devoted love, and exclaimed,—

" My own Astumastao ! "

Tucking her arm in his, as he had lately seen the white Christian people do, he proudly marched with her up to a prominent place in the audience, where they seated themselves, while the aunt for the present judiciously looked out for herself.

It was a very picturesque assembly. Indians dress in an endless variety of fashions. Some in their beautiful native costumes looked as statuesque and imposing as the ancient Greeks; others, as ridiculous as a modern dude. All were interested and filled with suppressed excitement. The first hour was spent in singing and prayer, and in reading the Word of God, or, as the Indians love to call it, the book of heaven.

Then the Indians who had come from Norway House with the missionary, and who were earnest Christians, told of how they had found the Saviour. Very clear and definite are many of the Christian Indians on this point. And as Paul loved to talk about how the Lord Jesus had met him while on the way to Damascus, so it is with many of these happy converted red men, they love to talk of their conversion.

To the great joy of the missionary, Oowikapun asked for the privilege of saying a few words. Of course it was granted. At first he seemed to falter a little, but he soon rose above all fear, and most blessedly and convincingly did he talk. We need not go over it again : it was the story of his life, as in these chapters it has been recorded. Because of the words and resolves of Astumastao, he said, he had gone for the missionary ; and from this man, and from Memotas and others, he had found the way of faith in the Son of God. Now he was trusting in Him with a

sweet belief that even he, Oowikapun, was a child of God, like
these other happy Christians who had spoken.

After such an hour of preliminary service, it was surely easy
for that missionary to preach. He took as his text the sixteenth
verse of the third chapter of John's Gospel.

Here is how it looks in Cree, which we give that our readers
may see what this beautiful language looks like :-

"Aspeeche saketat Kesa-Maneto askeeyou kah ke ooche maket
oopay ye-koo-sah-ke aweyit katapua yaye mah kwa akat keche
nese-wah nah-tee-sit maka kache at ayaky ka-ke-ka pimatisse-
win."

It was a long sermon that was preached that day. For long
hours that preacher talked without stopping. He had so much
to say, for here was a people who had never heard the gospel
before, and were now listening to it for the first time. Everything had to be made plain as he went along. He had to take
them back to the creation of the human family, and tell them of
the fall, and of the great plan of salvation to save the poor
sinning race who had wandered out of the right trail, and are
wandering in darkness and death, and bring them back again into
the right way, which has in it happiness for them here, and
heaven hereafter.

Thus the missionary talked, hour after hour, wishing to bring
them to a decision for Christ at once. He dwelt upon the great-
ness and impartiality of God's love; and urged them, that as His
love was so real and blessed, they should accept of Him now, at the
first great invitation.

The Spirit carried home to the hearts of these simple-hearted
people the truths uttered, and deep and genuine were the results.
After more singing and prayer, the preacher asked for some of
them to candidly tell what was in their hearts concerning these
truths, and what were their wishes and resolves, in reference to
becoming Christians.

To write down here all that was said that day would require
several more chapters. Suffice it to say, that from the chief, who
spoke first, through quite a succession of their best men, they were
all thankful for what they had heard, and said that these things

about the Great Spirit "satisfied their longing" and, as one put it, " filled up their hearts."

Thus the gospel reached Nelson river, and rapidly did it find a lodgment in the hearts of the people. At the close of the second service about forty men and women came forward to the front of the assembly and professed their faith in Christ, and desired Christian baptism, which had been explained to them. And thus the good work went on day after day, and many more decided fully for Christ.

Do not, my dear reader, say this work was too sudden, and that these baptisms were too soon. Nothing of the kind. It was only another chapter in the Acts of the Apostles, and in perfect harmony with what is recorded by infallible wisdom. There it is recorded of the multitudes after one sermon by Peter that "then they that gladly received his words were baptized, and the same day there were added unto them about three thousand souls."

CHAPTER XVII.

'WHILE SUPPER IS COOKING THE DOGS ARE GIVEN THEIR ONLY DAILY MEAL.'

CHAPTER XVII.

OF course Oowikapun and Astumastao were married. Everybody was invited, and, of course, everybody came to the wedding, and to the great feast that fo'lowed, and there was plenty of music, vocal and instrumental. Very kind and devoted was he to her, even like as Memotas had been to his wife.

The excitement of the arrival of the missionary after a time died away, but the good results continue to this day. Although at times slowly, yet constantly has the good work gone on, and none who at the beginning decided for the Christian life have ever gone back to the old pagan religion of their forefathers. So much had Oowikapun to say about Memotas, that he resolved, if possible, to see that blessed man once again. And to Astumastao also there came a longing desire to visit the spot to which now, more than ever, her memory turned, where that period, all too brief in her childhood days, had been spent, where in the home of the missionary, and in the house of God, she had learned the sweet lessons which had never entirely been forgotten, and which had, "after many days," produced such glorious results.

The longed for opportunity came the next summer, and was gladly accepted.

So successful had been the fur-hunters in their trapping the fur-bearing animals, such as the silver foxes, beavers, otters, minks, and others whose rich pelts are very valuable, that the Hudson Bay Trading Company resolved to send up to Norway

House a second brigade of boats to take up the surplus cargo left by the first brigade, and also to bring down a cargo of supplies for the extra trade, which was so rapidly developing.

Oowikapun was appointed steersman of one of the boats, and his wife was permitted to go with him.

With great delight were they both welcomed at Norway House Mission. They had had a long and dangerous trip. Many rapids had to be run, where the greatest skill was required in safely steering the little boats, but Oowikapun was alert and watchful, and did well. Twenty-five or thirty times did they have to make *portages* around the dangerous falls and rapids.

The joy of Astumastao on reaching the place where she had spent that eventful year, so long ago, was very great indeed. Absorbed in bringing up the memories of the past, she seemed at times like one in a dream. To find the playmates of that time, she had to search among those who now, like herself, had left the years of childhood far behind. Many of them had gone into the spirit land. Still she found a goodly number after a time, and great indeed was their mutual joy to renew the friendship of their earlier days. And great indeed was the pleasure of all to meet the wife of that Indian who had visited the mission in the depth of that cold winter, to plead for a missionary, especially when they learned that it was because of her earnest resolve, that he had undertaken the long, cold, dangerous journey.

They were welcome visitors at the Mission House. Sagasta-ookemow and Minnehaha seemed intuitively to love them, much to their delight, and as gravely listened, as did the older people, to the recital of some of the thrilling incidents of their lives. The services of the sanctuary were

"Seasons of sweet delight."

and in them much was learned, to be helpful in times to come.

Of course the little home of Memotas was visited. Their hearts were saddened at finding the one who for years had not only, as the missionary's most efficient helper, often ministered to the mind diseased, and brought comfort to the sin-sick soul, but had often, as in the case of Oowikapun, when bitten by the savage wolf, skilfully restored to health and vigour many suffering ones, now rapidly himself hastening to the tomb.

But although he was feeble in body he was joyous in spirit, and had the happy gift of making everybody happy who came to see him. Even in his last illness this remarkable man was a "son of consolation." For months ere he left us, he lived in an atmosphere of heaven, and longed for his eternal home. Only once after the arrival of Oowikapun and Astumastao did he have sufficient strength to go with them to the house of God. Every Indian within twenty miles of the sanctuary was there that bright Sabbath morning. Wan and pale, and *spirituel*, looked the saintly man who seemed to have, just by the strength of his will, kept the soul in the frail earthen vessel, that he might once again worship in the earthly sanctuary, ere he entered into that which is heavenly. When, with an effort, he raised himself up to speak, the place was indeed a Bochim, for the weepers were everywhere.

One illustration used by him has lingered with me through all these years. He said: " I am in body like the old wigwam that has been shaken by many a storm. Every additional blast that now assails it only makes the rents and crevices the more numerous and larger. *But the larger the breaks and openings, the more the sunshine can enter in.* So with me. Every pang of suffering, every trial of patience, only opens the way into my soul for more of Jesus and His love."

How he did rejoice as they talked with him, and rehearsed the story of how the Lord had so wonderfully led them out of the darkness of the old way into the blessed light of the new !

At Astumastao's request, Oowikapun told Memotas of his wonderful dream, and of the deep impression it had made upon him. Memotas listened to its recital with the deepest interest, and stated what many others have said, that they believed that still, as in ancient times, the Good Spirit in loving compassion speaks in dreams to help or warn those who have not yet received enough of the Divine revelation to be completely guided by it.

At his feet sat these two happy converts, and, as did many others, learned from his rich testimony many blessed truths.

Happy Memotas! only a little while longer did he tarry with us. A little additional cold was all that was needed to finish the work in a constitution so nearly shattered. When he felt it assailing him, there came very clearly to him the presentiment that the end was near; and never did a weary traveller welcome his home, and bed of rest, with greater delight than did Memotas welcome the grave, and the bliss beyond.

The prospect of getting to heaven seemed so glorious that he could hardly think of anything else. This was now his one absorbing thought.

Like all the rest of these northern Indians, he was very poor, and had nothing in his home for food of his own but fish. But there were loving hearts at the Mission House, and so willing hands carried supplies, as needed, to his little habitation.

On one occasion, when that dear, good missionary, the Rev. John Semmens, who was then with us and who had gone with me, as together we had lovingly supplied his wants, said to him : " Now, beloved Memotas, can we do anything else for you? Do you want anything more ? " " Oh no," replied Memotas, " I want nothing but Christ—more of Christ."

When we administered to him the emblems of the broken body and spilt blood of the dear Redeemer, he was much affected, and exclaimed, " My precious Saviour, I shall soon see Him ! "

Seeing his intense longing to go sweeping through the gates of the celestial city, I said to him, " Memotas, my brother beloved, why are you so anxious to leave us? I hope you will be spared to us a little longer. We need you in the church and in the village. We want your presence, your example, your prayers."

He was a little perplexed at first, and seemed hardly to know how to answer. Then he looked up at me so chidingly, and gave me the answer that outweighs all arguments, " I want to go home ! "

And Home he went, gloriously and triumphantly. His face was so radiant and shining, that it seemed to us as though the heavenly gates had swung back, and, from the glory land, some of its brightness had come flashing down, and had so illumined the poor body, that still held in its faltering grasp the precious soul, that we could almost imagine that mortal itself was putting on immortality.

The triumphant death of Memotas was not only a revelation and a benediction to Oowikapun and Astumastao, and many other Christian Indians, but it caused a full and complete surrender of many hard, stubborn hearts to Christ.

So short a time had our hero and heroine been in the way that, happy as they were in their present enjoyment of the favour of God, they had had their fears, as they thought, of the last enemy, which is Death. In the quietude of their wigwam home, they had asked themselves and each other the solemn question: Will this religion sustain us in the Valley of the Shadow of Death? or, How will we do in the swellings of Jordan? Natural and solemn are these questions, and wise and prudent are they, in all lands, who thoughtfully and reverently ask them.

Comforting and suggestive were the answers which they and others had learned at the bedside of the triumphant Memotas. "As thy day so shall thy strength be" had a new meaning to them from that time forward, and so, as they reconsecrated themselves to God, they resolved, in the Divine strength, to obtain each day sufficient grace for that day's needs—and who can do any better?

Very anxious was Astumastao to learn all she could about housekeeping, and other things, which would more fully fit her for helping her less fortunate Indian sisters at the distant Indian village, who, now that they had become Christians, were also trying to attain to some of the customs and comforts of civilisation.

Thus very quickly sped the few weeks away during which the brigade of boats waited at Norway House for their return cargo, which had to come from Fort Garry. When this arrived, all was hurry and excitement. Two or three days only were required to unpack from the large cases or bales the supplies and repack them in "pieces," as they are called in the language of the country. These "pieces" will each weigh from eighty to a hundred pounds. The cargoes are put up in this way on account of the many portages which have to be made, when the whole outfit has to be carried on the men's shoulders, supported by a strap from the forehead. It is laborious work, but these Indians are stalwart fellows, and now, being homeward bound, they worked with a will.

Most of them were at this time Christians. So they tarried at the mission for a little time to say "Farewell," and to take on board Astumastao, and two or three other Indian women, who had been wooed with such rapidity, that, ere the short visit of a few weeks rolled round, all arrangements had been made, and some pleasant little marriage ceremonies had taken place in our little church.

These marriages were a great joy to Astumastao, as her intensely practical character saw that the coming to her distant country of some genuine Christian young women, would be very helpful in the more rapid extension of Christianity. Indeed, "Dame Rumour," who lives there, as elsewhere, said that she had a good deal to do in introducing some of the shy, timid bachelor Indians of the Nelson river brigade, to some of the blushing damsels, whom she had, in her judgment, decided would make good wives for them, and also be a blessing in their new homes. Various amusing stories were flying about for a long time in reference to some of the queer misadventures, and mixing up of the parties concerned, ere everything was satisfactorily arranged and everybody satisfied. Among a people so primitive and simple in their habits, this could quickly be done, as no long months were required to arrange jointures, or marriage settlements, or a prying into the state of the bank accounts, of either of the parties concerned.

But all these things had been attended to, and the long journey began. It was a matter of thankfulness that no boats were smashed on the rocks, or lives lost in the raging waters. The women looked well after the cooking of the meals, and the mending of garments torn in the rough portages. Every morning and evening they read from the Good Book, and had prayers. Often in the long gloaming of those high latitudes, when the day's work was done, they clustered around the camp fire on the great smooth granite rocks, with the sparkling waters of lake or river in front, and the dense, dark forest as their background, and sweetly sang some of the sweet songs of Zion which they had lately learned, or were learning from these young Christian wives, whom the wise Astumastao had introduced among them.

The three Sabbaths which had to be spent on the journey were days of quiet restfulness and religious worship. It is a delightful fact that all of our northern Christian Indians rest from their huntings and journeyings on the Lord's Day. And it has been found, by many years of testing, that the Christian Indians who thus rest on the Sabbath, can do more, and better work, in these toilsome trips for the Hudson Bay Company, than those brigades that know no Sabbath.

The longest journey has an end. The far-away home was reached at last. The goods, in capital order, were handed over to the officer of the trading port. The men were paid for their work, and supplies were taken up for the winter's hunting, and one after another of the families dispersed to their different hunting grounds, some of which were hundreds of miles away.

Oowikapun, with Astumastao and her aunt, went with a number, whose wigwams were so arranged on their hunting grounds, that they could meet frequently for religious worship among themselves. Very blessed and helpful to them was this little church in the wilderness.

And now we must for the present leave them. They had their trials and sorrows, as all have. Even if their home was but a wigwam, it was a happy one, with its family altar and increasing joys.

They have never become weary of talking about the wonderful way in which their loving Heavenly Father has led them out of the dark path of the old life into this blessed way.

The only question on which they differed was, which had had more to do in bringing in the gospel to their people. Astumastao said it was the visit of Oowikapun; while he declared that if it had not been for her true brave life and faithful words, and her endeavour to live up to what light she had received when a little child, they might all have been in darkness still. And I think my readers will believe with me that Oowikapun was right, when he so emphatically argued that to Astumastao, more than to any one else, was to be given this high honour.

So, while in our story we have given Oowikapun such a prominent place, yet to Astumastao, we think our dear readers with us will say, must be given the first place among those who have been instrumental in having the gospel introduced among the Nelson River Indians.

Printed by Hazell, Watson, & Viney, Ld., London and Aylesbury.

BY THE SAME AUTHOR.

BY CANOE AND DOG-TRAIN AMONG THE CREE AND SALTEAUX INDIANS.

Introduction by Rev. MARK GUY PEARSE.

FIFTEENTH THOUSAND.

With Woodburytype Portraits of the REV. E. R. YOUNG *and* MRS. YOUNG. *Map, and Thirty-two Illustrations.* **3s. 6d.**

"As we turn page after page of this book, we meet with crisp and even, humorous incidents, thrilling escapes, privations patiently borne, graphic sketches of native life and character, and, best of all, evidences on all hands of the power of the Gospel of the Lord Jesus Christ."—*Illustrated Missionary News.*

"Young and old will read this amazing story with delight. His heroic journeys through the snow are described in a way that will secure the attention of all."—*Sword and Trowel.*

"A more interesting and delightful book I have not read for many a day."—*Good Company.*

"One of the most fascinating volumes of Missionary adventure published in our time."—*Methodist Free Churches Magazine.*

"One of the most thrilling narratives of Missionary life and adventure ever published."—*Birmingham Daily Gazette.*

"Even readers who have not the 'smallest sympathy with Foreign Missionary work may follow with interest this simple, straightforward, unvarnished narrative of a life of thrilling adventure and heroic endurance."—*Literary World.*

"Ought to be almost as fascinating as 'Robinson Crusoe' itself, to such as like stories of wild, and sometimes dangerous adventure, to enliven their evenings by the fireside."—*Scots Magazine.*

"The boys, especially, will have a ready ear for the adventures with canoes and dog-trains, whilst all the time they will be within sound of the Gospel music with which the book is filled."—*Divine Life.*

'It is a marvellously interesting story of heroic adventure."—*Methodist New Connexion Magazine.*

LONDON:

CHARLES H. KELLY, 2, CASTLE STREET, CITY ROAD, E.C.,

AND

66, PATERNOSTER ROW, E.C.

STORIES FROM INDIAN WIGWAMS AND NORTHERN CAMP FIRES.

SEVENTH THOUSAND.

Forty-three Illustrations. Imperial 16mo. **3s. 6d.**

"Mr. Young here gives another happy combination of adventurous narrative, graphic description, humour, detailed information about the Indians. and a record of earnest, self-denying missionary work."—*London Missionary Chronicle.*

"The stirring tales of adventure in the wild north land contained in this handsome volume will interest all the boys, and many who have outgrown boyhood. . . . Romance and travel combine to make the narrative an enthralling one."—*Manchester Courier.*

"Mr. Young's stories are not only smartly written. but they are exciting to a degree, and far more entertaining than many a popular novel."—*Lincolnshire Free Press.*

"A more entertaining record of travel is not easily found. . . . The stories of wild life, the folk-lore of vanished tribes, the stirring incidents of the hunter's or trapper's career, make up an eminently readable book. It conveys a vivid impression of a wild life, which year by year loses some of its peculiar characteristics."—*Leeds Mercury.*

"A unique book of Missionary adventure. Stories, hairbreadth escapes, and adventurous journeys, in all seasons and amid all kinds of scenery, are here recorded, with a modesty, a humour, and a spiritual earnestness, that will delight young and old. Truly an instructive and delightful book."—*Scottish Geographical Magazine.*

"We can speak of this book with unqualified approval. The idea given of the Indians—their life, warfare, oratory, the kind of Christians they make—is unusually vivid and interesting."—*The Presbyterian.*

"One of the most fascinating, instructive, and stimulating of modern Missionary books."—DR. A. T. PIERSON.

LONDON :

CHARLES H. KELLY, 2, CASTLE STREET, CITY ROAD, E.C.,

AND

66, PATERNOSTER ROW, E.C.